90 DAYS BIBLE READING GUIDE

GUIDANCE

MANY THANKS TO THE ORIGINAL *AM/PM* TEAM, TO JOHN BUCKERIDGE FOR ACTING AS CONSULTANT EDITOR, TO PHIL WASON AND PAUL FENTON FOR THEIR ADVICE AND SUPPORT AND TO PHIL JONES AT MARKETING FX FOR HIS DESIGN.

ACKNOWLEDGEMENTS

DAYZD

90 DAYS BIBLE READING GUIDE

GUIDANCE

a SUbtle publication for

Scripture
Union

Scripture Union
207–209 Queensway, Bletchley
Milton Keynes MK2 2EB.

Cover design and internal design
by Marketing FX

First Published 1996, reprinted
2000, 2001, 2002

British Library Cataloguing-in-
publication Data.
A catalogue record for this book
is available from the British
Library.

ISBN 1 85999 154 8

Printed in Great Britain by
Ebenezer Baylis & Son Limited
The Trinity Press, Worcester, and
London.

CONFUSED?

start here!

DAYZD is a Bible Reading Guide that you can start whenever you like and read wherever you like!

DAYZD gets to the heart of what the Bible says about *guidance*. It won't give you all the theological answers, but it will encourage you to think about what the Bible says for yourself.

What to do?

• *Pray before you start.* If you ask God to speak to you as you use DAYZD he will!

• *Read the Bible passage.* Ask yourself: What is the main point of the passage? What does the Bible passage say about God? Have I learnt something new about myself? Is there a promise or a warning to take notice of?

• *Read DAYZD.*

• *Make notes.* There is some space on each page to jot down any thoughts or comments you have on the passage.

• *Pray.* After you have finished each study, talk to God about how you feel and what you have learnt.

• *Action.* Check out the 'Action' section which includes prayer ideas, song lyrics to meditate on, worship ideas, books to read and quotes to think about.

• *Tick box.* On each page there is a small 'tick box'. When you feel you have completed a page, tick the box. This will help you remember where you are in your DAYZD Bible Reading Guide.

• *DAYZD is based on the Good News Bible, but can be used with other Bible translations.*

CHECK OUT

PSALM 25

TO KNOW GOD'S WILL, WE HAVE TO TALK AND LISTEN TO HIM. ONE WAY OF DOING THIS IS THROUGH PRAYER. WHAT IS THE BEST WAY TO COME TO GOD IN PRAYER? THIS PSALM GIVES YOU A GOOD MODEL.

THE BEST WAY.

Look at yourself.

• 'Help me!' (vs 1-3). Talk to God about what is bothering you.
• 'Guide me' (vs 4,5). Prayer is about letting God sort you out.
• 'Forgive me' (vs 6,7). God promises to forgive us. Read and try to learn 1 John 1:9.

Look at God.

When you pray it helps if you think about the nature of God you're praying to. This psalm lists some things that are true of God, and what that means for you.

Make a list of the characteristics of God described here and what that means for you, eg in verse 8: God is righteous and good and that means he guides and leads us (vs 8-10).

Thank God that, because he's the kind of God he is, he accepts you as the sort of person you are.

ACTION

• IS THERE AN AREA IN YOUR LIFE IN WHICH YOU NEED GOD TO HELP AND GUIDE YOU? USING PSALM 25 AS A BASIS FOR PRAYER, TAKE EACH SECTION AND READ IT OUT. AFTER THE FIRST SECTION MEDITATE ON THE WORDS YOU HAVE JUST SPOKEN. NOW MOVE ON TO THE NEXT SECTION, READING IT ALOUD AND THEN THINKING ABOUT THE WORDS YOU HAVE PRAYED. CARRY ON UNTIL YOU HAVE REACHED THE END OF THE PSALM. TRUST THAT GOD HAS HEARD YOUR PRAYER AND HE WILL ANSWER IT.

1 CHRONICLES 29:10-20

DAVID AND HIS PEOPLE HAVE JUST GOT TOGETHER THE MONEY, THE PLANS AND THE MATERIALS TO BUILD THE TEMPLE. GOD HAD TOLD DAVID THAT HE WASN'T TO BUILD THE TEMPLE HIMSELF, BUT THAT HIS SON SOLOMON WAS TO COMPLETE IT. NOW STAGE ONE IS OVER, AND DAVID IS THRILLED AT THE WAY IT HAS ALL COME TOGETHER. SO HE AND ALL THE PEOPLE STOP TO THANK GOD.

STAGE ONE IS OVER.

Think about your own life. When you are pleased about the success of something, whom do you congratulate first?

What have you got to thank God for? Stop for a moment and list a few things either in your head or on paper.

Remember

• God is king of the universe (v 11). Nothing is outside his control.
• Nobody succeeds or fails without God allowing it to happen (v 12).
• We can't give God anything – everything we have is a gift from him (v 14).
• We are totally dependent upon God for everything (vs 15,16).

Spend a few moments thinking about the descriptions of God in this passage. Which of them means most to you today?

ACTION

• BEFORE STARTING TO PRAY, THINK ABOUT HOW READING THIS PASSAGE IS GOING TO CHANGE YOUR ATTITUDE TOWARDS GIVING THANKS TO GOD?

1 CHRONICLES 17:16-27

THIS PASSAGE FLASHES BACK TO AN EARLIER TIME IN DAVID'S LIFE. THE PROPHET NATHAN HAS JUST TOLD DAVID THAT HIS KINGDOM WILL GROW STRONG AND HIS SON WILL BE KING AFTER HIM.

AN EARLIER TIME.

David immediately sits down to thank God and to pray about his life and the course it's taking. Try working through the prayer, picking out features of the way David prays which will help you to pray:

• He's humble (v 16).
• He's chatty (v 18).
• He's reverent (v 20).
• He remembers God's goodness in the past (vs 21,22).
• He prays specifically about a promise from God (vs 23-26).
• He gives reasons for his request (vs 24,25).

Pray about your life in the year ahead, basing your prayer on David's model.

How did God keep his promise to preserve David's dynasty for all time (v 24)? (Check out Luke 1:67-72 for extra help.)

ACTION

• HAS GOD MADE A COMMITMENT TO GUIDE YOU THROUGH YOUR LIFE? SPEND SOME TIME IN PRAYER THANKING GOD FOR THE GUIDANCE HE HAS ALREADY GIVEN IN YOUR LIFE AND PRAY FOR REASSURANCE THAT HE IS GOING TO BE THERE IN THE FUTURE AS WELL.

CHECK OUT
PSALM 146

PEOPLE WE LOOK UP TO.

MOST OF US HAVE HEROES – OR AT LEAST PEOPLE WE LOOK UP TO – BUT VERSE 3 WARNS AGAINST DEPENDING ON HEROES OR GREAT LEADERS. THE PSALMIST SAYS WE SHOULDN'T PUT OUR TRUST IN THEM. ONLY GOD IS WORTHY OF THAT. OR, AS THE AMERICAN SHOPKEEPER PUT IT, 'IN GOD WE TRUST; EVERYBODY ELSE PAYS CASH.'

Look at verses 7-9 of this psalm. If God is like that, what should we as his followers be doing?

Think of practical ways in which your church or fellowship could reflect God's attitudes as we see them here. Here are two suggestions – add your own to the list

'The Lord sets prisoners free':
Visit a house-bound pensioner.

'The Lord gives food to the hungry':
Raise money for famine relief.

ACTION

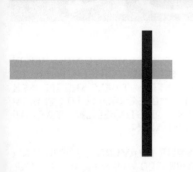

• MOST OF US CAN REMEMBER TIMES WHEN WE HAVE BEEN LET DOWN: BY BOY/GIRLFRIENDS, PARENTS, FRIENDS, TEACHERS. IN FACT ANYONE WHO CANNOT LIVE UP TO OUR EXPECTATIONS. IT'S HARD TO TRUST AGAIN WHEN YOU HAVE BEEN LET DOWN. ASK GOD TO HELP YOU TRUST HIM. HE IS PERFECT. HE CANNOT LET US DOWN.

DAYZD 4

PSALM 107:1-32

THE FIRST HALF OF THIS PSALM IS IN FOUR SECTIONS - ALL ABOUT GOD'S PEOPLE IN TROUBLE AND IN NEED OF GUIDANCE: TRAVELLERS (VS 4-9); PRISONERS (VS 10-16); THOSE WHO WERE ILL (VS 17-22); SEAFARERS (VS 23-32).

PEOPLE IN TROUBLE.

There's a pattern to the way in which God deals with them. It goes:

1. Distress, followed by,
2. Prayer, followed by,
3. Rescue, followed by,
4. Thanksgiving.

Think of ways in which God has answered prayer for you recently. Have you thanked him for the answers? If you can't think of any answers you've received, could it be because:

• you've not asked for help (v 6)?
• you've asked for your way instead of God's (v 11)?
• your requests were so vague you can't recognise when they're answered?
• you've forgotten to watch for the answers?

ACTION

• PRAY SPECIFICALLY FOR SOMEONE YOU KNOW WHO'S IN TROUBLE. ASK GOD TO HELP THEM TO GET OUT OF THE SITUATION THEY ARE IN. ASK GOD TO MAKE THEM HUMBLE ENOUGH TO COME TO HIM FOR HELP, INSTEAD OF STRUGGLING TO DEAL WITH THEIR SITUATION ALONE.

• KEEP A NOTE OF YOUR PRAYERS SO YOU CAN LOOK BACK AND THANK GOD WHEN HE ANSWERS!

DAYZD 5

PSALM 7

SERIOUS DANGER.

WHEN WE TALK TO GOD, THERE'S ONLY ONE BASIS ON WHICH WE CAN COME TO HIM - AS FORGIVEN SINNERS. HERE THE PSALMIST PROTESTS HIS INNOCENCE (V 8) AND ASKS GOD TO PROTECT HIM FROM THE WICKED WHO ARE AFTER HIM. THAT DOESN'T MEAN HE'S PERFECT, OR HAS NEVER DONE ANYTHING WRONG. ROMANS 3:23 MAKES IT CLEAR THAT NOBODY EXCEPT JESUS FALLS INTO THAT CATEGORY.

But when we come to God, through Jesus, he puts us right (Romans 5:1; the *New International Version* of the Bible has 'justified', *The Contemporary English Version* has 'By faith we have been made acceptable to God'). Then he protects us, and rescues us (v 1), though not necessarily in the way we expect. Maybe he'll protect us from bitterness or fear, or give us love and peace right in the middle of some horrible situation.

'Justice' and 'righteousness' are the same word in Hebrew. Go through the psalm and pick out the number of times those ideas occur. What does that emphasise about God?

Check out verses 14-16. Think about the times you set out to do things to hurt people (not just physically, mentally as well). Ask God to forgive you for those times. It may help if you write them down on a piece of paper and go through the list.

ACTION

• MOST OF US DO NOT LIVE IN FEAR FOR OUR LIVES, BUT FOR SOME PEOPLE FOLLOWING GOD MEANS SERIOUS DANGER. VERSE 1 OF PSALM 7 TELLS US THAT GOD IS THE PERSON TO GO TO IF WE NEED PROTECTION. IF YOU KNOW OF MISSIONARIES ABROAD, PRAY FOR THEM NOW. ASK FOR GOD'S PROTECTION AND GUIDANCE IN THEIR LIVES.

DAYZD 6

CHECK OUT
MARK 7:24-30

WHAT WAS JESUS TALKING ABOUT IN VERSE 27?

THE WOMAN WAS A GENTILE - A NON-JEW.
JESUS PROBABLY QUOTED A SAYING THAT
WAS AROUND AT THE TIME (OR MAYBE HE
MADE IT UP HIMSELF) TO SEE HOW THE
WOMAN WOULD REACT.

MAYBE HE MADE IT
UP HIMSELF?

'Feeding the children' meant looking after the Jewish people.

'Throwing food to the dogs' meant wasting God's love on people who were supposed to be beyond God's care.

He is asking the woman, in effect, 'Look, everyone thinks I shouldn't help you, because you're a Gentile. What do you think?'

And the woman comes back and says 'Even Gentiles can receive God's love.'

Jesus says 'Great – that's just the sort of faith God wants.'

And her daughter is healed.

• What problem are you facing?
• What is Jesus asking you to believe?

Talking to God is okay when things are going well. But what if they aren't? For the next four studies we'll be looking at how we can be honest with God.

ACTION

• IN THIS PASSAGE WE SEE ONE WAY IN
WHICH GOD GUIDED AND HELPED PEOPLE IN
THE PAST - THROUGH JESUS' TEACHINGS.
WE STILL HAVE JESUS' TEACHINGS TODAY
IN THE BIBLE. DO YOU SPEND ENOUGH TIME READING YOUR BIBLE AND
PRAYING TO GOD? MAKE SURE YOU SET SOME TIME ASIDE ON A
REGULAR BASIS TO GET TO KNOW GOD.

MARK 9:14-29

THE DISCIPLES FELT CONFUSED. THEY THOUGHT GOD HAD GIVEN THEM THE POWER TO HEAL AND THEY COULDN'T UNDERSTAND WHAT HAD GONE WRONG. BUT THEY BROUGHT THEIR PROBLEM TO JESUS: 'WHY COULDN'T WE DRIVE THE SPIRIT OUT?'

CONFUSED?

The man felt helpless. He was afraid Jesus wasn't strong enough to heal his son. But he came to Jesus with his problem.

And Jesus said:

• God has all the power in the world: 'Everything is possible ...' (v 23).
• Believe this: '... for the person who has faith' (v 23).
• Don't depend on yourselves: 'Only prayer ... nothing else' (v 29).

GOOD NEWS: 'As our faith is never perfect, it follows that we are partly unbelievers; but God forgives us and reckons us believers on account of a small portion of faith.' *John Calvin.*

Which of these do you think are true?
• God wants us to pray and to try hard to have enough faith.
• God doesn't want us to pray unless we've got enough faith.
• God wants us to pray even if our faith is really small.

'Faith isn't faith until it's all you're holding on to.'

ACTION

• WHEN WE ARE GOING THROUGH TOUGH TIMES, GOD GUIDES US BACK TO HIM. IF YOU ARE GOING THROUGH A TESTING TIME AT THE MOMENT, COME BACK TO WHERE GOD IS. WE ARE THE ONES THAT WANDER OFF COURSE AND LOSE SIGHT OF HIM.

JOB 10:1-17, 14:13-17

CAN YOU TELL GOD EXACTLY HOW YOU'RE FEELING? JOB DID. HE'D BEEN THROUGH AN AWFUL TIME - HE'D LOST HIS FLOCKS, HIS POSSESSIONS AND THEN HIS CHILDREN. HE'D ALSO BEEN RAVAGED BY DISEASE AND WAS LEFT WITH A TERRIBLE SKIN COMPLAINT. EVEN HIS FRIENDS WERE NO USE. BUT AFTER ALL HE'D BEEN THROUGH, HE STILL HAD FAITH IN GOD THOUGH HE DIDN'T LIKE WHAT GOD WAS ALLOWING TO HAPPEN TO HIM. IN FACT, HE WAS STRESSED OUT AND WOUND UP AND WHO COULD BLAME HIM!

AN AWFUL TIME.

Being faithful to God didn't mean that he couldn't be honest with God. Put in your own words some of the things Job says to God. Check out these verses: 10:1,2,4-6,14-17.

Now stop and write down how you're feeling at the moment. Make it into a prayer. Maybe there's something that's really winding you up just now – tell God about it!

Job was honest about his anger – God heard him and helped him cope by giving him hope for the future (14:13-17).

Being angry isn't always wrong – see Ephesians 4:26.

ACTION

• IT HELPS SOMETIMES WHEN WE ARE ANGRY TO SIT QUIETLY AND RELAX. IT'S HARD TO TALK THINGS THROUGH WITH GOD WHEN ALL YOUR THOUGHTS ARE JUMBLED IN YOUR HEAD. PLAY SOME RELAXING MUSIC IF IT HELPS AND MEDITATE ON THE BIBLE VERSES. BE HONEST WITH GOD THOUGH AND TELL HIM EXACTLY HOW YOU FEEL. ASK FOR HIS HELP TO DEAL WITH THE ANGER.

JEREMIAH 20:7-13

IS IT WRONG TO GET DEPRESSED? JEREMIAH HAD BEEN THROUGH A LOT SINCE HE WAS CALLED TO BE A PROPHET. HE'D BEEN RIDICULED, IMPRISONED, CURSED AND BEATEN. HE WAS DEPRESSED, AND HE HAD GOOD REASON TO BE. SO HE TOLD GOD ABOUT:

DEPRESSED?

• how it felt (vs 14,17).
• how hard his message was to preach (v 8).
• how impossible it was for him to give up being a prophet (v 9).
• how he longed for God to take revenge (v 12).

He said exactly how he felt. And God heard him, and understood.

Bring to God the difficult things you've got to do this week that get you down. Also pray for other people who are feeling down, especially if they're being laughed at for doing what God wants.

ACTION

• IT IS HARD FOR US TO UNDERSTAND WHY GOD ALLOWS US TO GO THROUGH THINGS WHICH WE FIND TOUGH. PERHAPS IT IS BECAUSE WE CANNOT SEE THE OVERALL PLAN HE HAS FOR OUR LIVES?

CHECK OUT VERSE 13. IT SEEMS AN ODD THING FOR SOMEONE TO SAY WHO IS FEELING ANGRY OR DEPRESSED. WE ARE TO WORSHIP GOD NO MATTER HOW WE FEEL. WHY NOT LISTEN TO A WORSHIP SONG NOW.

ASK GOD TO RESCUE YOU FROM THE POWER OF EVIL PEOPLE.

CHECK OUT
NUMBERS 11:10-23

ELEVEN

IT WAS OVER TWO YEARS SINCE MOSES HAD LED THE PEOPLE OF GOD OUT OF EGYPT, AND THEY WERE MOANING. 'THE FOOD'S NO GOOD - ALL WE GET IS MANNA, AND THERE'S NEVER ANY MEAT.'

THE FOOD'S NO GOOD.

Moses had had enough: 'Come on, God! I didn't come out here to be a wet-nurse to this bunch of whingers. I'm fed up with leading them. All they do is give me stick. I'd rather be dead than carry on leading this lot' (vs 11-15).

God answered Moses' honest cry for help (vs 16-18), but the people's godless grumbling brought tragedy (vs 20,33).

Are you sometimes involved in leading a Christian group? How do you feel when the group members moan, 'Boring!' Remember – next time it happens, take your feelings straight to God. Don't be spiteful towards the individuals concerned.

Satan hates it when God uses people to spread his word. He will try anything to stop that happening – the easiest way he can do this is by turning Christians against Christians. Ask God to give you the strength not to be used in this way.

ACTION

• 'GOD CAN TURN STUMBLING BLOCKS INTO STEPPING STONES.'

• GOD'S WORDS IN VERSE 23 ARE SIMILAR TO THE WORDS OF JESUS IN MARK 9:23. WHY DON'T WE PRAY MORE OFTEN, MORE SERIOUSLY AND MORE HONESTLY? START TODAY!

DAYZD 11

2 KINGS 20:1-11

HEZEKIAH HAS SERVED GOD FAITHFULLY. WHEN ISAIAH GIVES HIM GOD'S MESSAGE THAT HE WILL DIE HIS GRIEF LEADS HIM TO PRAY (V 3). GOD GRANTS HIM FIFTEEN MORE YEARS, AND PROMISES TO RESCUE JERUSALEM FROM ITS ENEMIES (V 6).

But Hezekiah wants a sign to prove this will happen. We don't know exactly what God did here. What is clear is that he gave Hezekiah the sign he asked for (v 9).

Did Hezekiah really need the sign – or would God have answered anyway?

Isn't it amazing that when we pray, God not only hears but acts. He never says 'go away I'm busy', or 'this isn't a good time at the moment'. He is the ever-attentive parent.

Pray for God to reveal his goodness and love in the life of someone you know who is ill.

GOD'S MESSAGE.

ACTION

• DOES IT MEAN THAT PEOPLE WHO ARE NOT HEALED HAVEN'T BEEN PRAYED FOR ENOUGH OR GOD DOESN'T LOVE THEM? NOT AT ALL! GOD HAS A PLAN FOR EACH OF US. SOMETIMES HE REVEALS FRAGMENTS OF THOSE PLANS, SOMETIMES HE DOESN'T. WHAT WE DO KNOW IS GOD WORKS FOR THE BEST OF EACH OF US. CHECK OUT *WHAT ABOUT IT?* BY LANCE PIERSON, SCRIPTURE UNION. HE LOOKS AT THE QUESTIONS WHICH PUZZLE PEOPLE AND ANSWERS THEM IN AN UNDERSTANDABLE WAY.

CHECK OUT

GENESIS 18:16-33

HAVE YOU EVER FELT THAT YOU CAN'T ASK GOD SOMETHING?

THIS PASSAGE SAYS: ASK GOD ANYWAY, AND KEEP ON TALKING TO HIM. HE WON'T LAUGH, OR TELL YOU OFF, OR IGNORE YOU. IF YOU'RE HONEST WITH GOD AND REALLY CARE, HE'LL KEEP ON HELPING YOU STEP BY STEP, UNTIL LIKE ABRAHAM, YOU KNOW WHAT TO PRAY FOR.

KEEP ON TALKING.

Prayer is not about God changing his mind. It's about God teaching us to get our will in line with his will. For Abraham that took time – and attention – as he gained confidence from God's answers.

Often we pray that God's will be done – for him to guide us in the way he knows best. But do we really listen to him? It's easy to come to prayer with an agenda already set, eg 'I want to go out with Carl and if God really loves me he will allow it to happen'. We have already decided that we know better than God.

ACTION

• CHECK OUT MATTHEW 6:5-13. USE IT AS A BASIS TO PRAY NOW. READ EACH VERSE CAREFULLY AND PAUSE FOR A SHORT WHILE AFTER EACH VERSE, THINKING ABOUT WHAT THE WORDS MEAN.

IF YOU REALLY WANT GOD TO GUIDE YOU, ALLOW HIM TO!

DAYZD 13

2 CHRONICLES 1:1-12

THIS OR THAT?

THERE ARE TIMES WHEN WE PRAY AND ARE REALLY PUZZLED ABOUT WHAT WE SHOULD ASK FOR. SHOULD I DO THIS OR THAT EXAM, TAKE THIS JOB, GO ON THAT HOLIDAY, SPEND MY MONEY ON THIS OR THAT?

Solomon had it sussed. Of all the things he could have asked for, he chose wisdom and knowledge (v 10). And God was pleased because wisdom would make him the king God wanted him to be.

God promises to help us when we don't know what to do or how to pray.

Look up:
• James 1:5.
• Romans 8:26,27.

Pray for someone you know who needs to make the right choices.

Wisdom is the ability to hear what God wants and see how to apply it. It is one of the gifts of the Spirit (1 Corinthians 12:8) – so why not ask for it!

ACTION

• CHECK OUT MATTHEW 7:7-11. THESE VERSES ARE A REAL ENCOURAGEMENT TO CHRISTIANS. DOES THAT MEAN IF YOU ASK FOR A CAR GOD WILL PROVIDE IT? GOD PROVIDES US WITH ALL WE NEED NOT NECESSARILY WITH WHAT WE WANT.

CHECK OUT

EPHESIANS 3:14-21 & 1 TIMOTHY 2:1-4

HOW DO YOU KNOW WHAT TO ASK FOR WHEN YOU PRAY?

WHEN YOU'RE PRAYING FOR OTHER PEOPLE, IT'S QUITE LIKELY YOU'LL RUN OUT OF THINGS TO SAY. 'GOD BLESS ALICE, GOD BLESS ADAM' IS A BIT BORING - BOTH FOR YOU AND GOD! HOW ABOUT USING PAUL'S PRAYER TO STIR THE IMAGINATION?

STIR THE IMAGINATION?

What does he ask for the Ephesian Christians? Check out verses 16-19.

Maybe you can't use Paul's high-flown language, but you can ask God to fill Alice with his love for her mum, and to give Adam the power to cope with his mates taking the mickey out of him at work.

It's not too easy, either, to know how to pray for the world around us. Again, take Paul's example in 1 Timothy 2.

Who should we pray for? (vs 1,2).
What should we pray for (v 2).
Why should we pray it? (vs 3,4).

ACTION

• WATCH A TV NEWS BULLETIN, THEN SPEND SOME TIME PRAYING ABOUT THE PEOPLE FEATURED ON THE NEWS.

• ALTERNATIVELY ASK YOUR CHURCH WHETHER YOU CAN RECEIVE A COPY OF A PRAYER LETTER FROM A MISSIONARY YOUR CHURCH SUPPORTS. MAKE SURE THAT YOU PRAY REGULARLY FOR THAT PERSON.

DAYZD 15

EPHESIANS 5:19,20 & PSALM 116

SIXTEEN **16**

DON'T JUST SING!

WHAT SHOULD WE DO WHEN GOD ANSWERS OUR PRAYERS? PRAISE HIM!

DON'T JUST SING TO GOD IN CHURCH! TRY OTHER PLACES TOO - THOUGH IT MAY NOT BE ALL THAT WISE TO BREAK OUT INTO A WORSHIP SONG IF YOUR FAMILY WILL THINK YOU'VE GONE BANANAS!

PSALM 116 IS ALL ABOUT SOMEONE WHO'S BEEN SAVED FROM DEATH GOING TO THE TEMPLE TO GIVE THANKS TO GOD. WHAT DOES PAUL TELL THE CHRISTIANS IN EPHESUS TO GIVE THANKS FOR?

You could try thanking God as you:

• take a walk in the countryside or a park;
• keep a notebook with two columns, one for prayer and one for the answers as they come;
• think of one or two specific answers to prayer and write a psalm following the style of Psalm 116;
• concentrate on one person you love or one aspect of your life and think of everything good about that person or activity;
• sing some worship songs – try using a praise tape to sing with, eg Spring Harvest, Songs of Fellowship New Songs;
• play a musical instrument;
• any other ideas?

ACTION

• CHECK OUT *DAYZD: WORSHIP*, FOR MORE IDEAS ON WORSHIPPING GOD.

• WHAT ABOUT TIMES WHEN IT SEEMS THAT YOUR PRAYERS HAVEN'T BEEN ANSWERED? GOD ALWAYS ANSWERS OUR PRAYERS, BUT HE DOES IT IN HIS TIME AND IN A WAY THAT HE KNOWS IS BEST FOR US. WE SHOULD STILL WORSHIP GOD.

DAYZD 16

PSALMS 122-124

THERE ARE TIMES WHEN IT IS HARD TO PRAY ON YOUR OWN, AND THAT MAKES YOU FEEL LOW. BUT GOD ALSO HEARS US WHEN WE PRAY WITH OTHER PEOPLE (SEE WHAT JESUS PROMISES IN MATTHEW 18:19,20), AND THAT'S A GOOD WAY TO SUSTAIN OUR PRAYING WHEN NOTHING ELSE SEEMS TO WORK. (IT'S NOT A SUBSTITUTE FOR PRIVATE PRAYER, BUT IT CAN BE A HELP.)

IT IS HARD TO PRAY ON YOUR OWN.

Write down or think of your own heading to each of these three psalms:

Psalm 122

• It's good to worship God together (v 1).
• It's good to pray for each other together (vs 6-9)

Psalm 123

• Sometimes we need to pray together for God to have pity on us.

Psalm 124

• It's exciting to share with other Christians in a particular prayer that God will act in a situation.

ACTION

• WHY NOT MAKE UP A PRAYER TRIPLET WITH TWO OTHER PEOPLE? MEET REGULARLY TO PRAY FOR YOUR FAMILIES, YOUR FRIENDS, YOUR SCHOOL, ETC USING THE HINTS FROM TODAY'S PSALMS TO HELP YOU.

• GOD CAN USE OTHER CHRISTIANS TO SPEAK TO YOU. PRAY THAT HE WILL AND THAT YOU WILL BE WILLING TO LISTEN TO THEM.

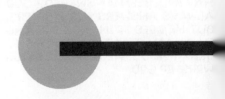

2 SAMUEL 6:12-23

WE TALK TO GOD IN A LOT OF DIFFERENT MOODS AND
GOD GUIDES US IN LOTS OF DIFFERENT WAYS. LOOK
BACK OVER THE LAST FEW STUDIES TO SEE HOW
GOD'S PEOPLE SHARE ALL THEIR FEELINGS
WITH THE GOD WHO CARES ABOUT THEM
AND LOVES THEM AS A TRUE FATHER.

This last passage shows David making a fool of himself (v 14). Why? – because he's enjoying worshipping God!

DIFFERENT MOODS.

Michal couldn't cope with the king behaving like that (see vs 16,20). She's critical of David. She doesn't see that true worship – enjoying a relationship with God – is what's behind David's actions.

This passage is often quoted in arguments about dancing in church. What's important is the attitude that lies behind worship (see v 21).

Read John 4:23,24. Does it matter if you look like a wally if you're worshipping God? No easy answers here!

ACTION

• READ THIS POEM. DO YOU EVER FEEL LIKE THIS IS GOD'S PRESENCE?

WOULD I DANCE?
WOULD I DANCE?
SURE I WOULD!
AND I DID.
MY HEART THROBBED
TO YOUR RHYTHM, LORD,
WHEN YOU ASKED ME TO DANCE.
YOUR MUSIC STILL PLAYS,
AND MY LIFE STILL SWAYS
IN PRAISE,
MY LORD,
IN PRAISE.

HALCYON BACKHOUSE

CHECK OUT

EXODUS 1:6-22

JOSEPH IS FORGOTTEN. BY HIS SKILFUL ORGANISATION HE HAS SAVED THE EGYPTIANS FROM STARVATION. BUT THAT WAS A LONG TIME AGO. THE NEW KING PANICS AND COMES UP WITH TWO DRASTIC STRATEGIES.

TWO DRASTIC STRATEGIES.

'Help! The place is full of foreigners!

Let's keep them down by
• putting them in labour-camps (vs 11-14)
• killing their baby boys (vs 15-22).

But the king soon learns that there can be no standing in the way of God's plan. You can try, but it won't have a long-term effect!

Can you identify two sentences in this reading which suggest that the king's desperate measures were useless?

In a new way, Christians are God's people now, and ultimately no one can spoil God's plan for them. That's why Paul is full of hope when things look grim (Ephesians 1:9-12). Spend time thanking God that you are included in those verses.

ACTION

• 'WE ARE OFTEN TROUBLED, BUT NOT CRUSHED; SOMETIMES IN DOUBT, BUT NEVER IN DESPAIR; MANY ENEMIES, BUT NEVER WITHOUT A FRIEND; AND THOUGH BADLY HURT AT TIMES, BUT NOT DESTROYED.' 2 CORINTHIANS 4:8,9.

GIVE THANKS TO GOD, THAT EVEN THOUGH PEOPLE MAY TRY AND STOP HIS PLANS, GOD WILL NOT ALLOW THEM TO.

EXODUS 2:1-25

REBEL FOR GOD.

WHY DON'T YOU BE A REBEL FOR GOD - BUT, LIKE MOSES, BE A REBEL WITH A CAUSE (HEBREWS 11:23-27).

AND EVEN REBELS NEED TO BE TRAINED! MOSES' TRAINING STARTED IN THE FLOATING BASKET AND CONTINUED FOR ABOUT FORTY YEARS BEFORE HE BEGAN HIS MAJOR LIFE'S WORK FOR GOD.

He had to be trained in:
• life in the Egyptian palace (Acts 7:20-22).
• midianite desert life (including the organisation of tribes and shepherding, Exodus 3:1).
• love for his own people (2:11,12).

Why were each of these early phases so important in the training of Moses?

Moses thought he was being a rebel, but it was all part of God's plan.

ACTION

• WHAT IS GOD TRAINING YOU FOR? THE EXPERIENCES YOU GO THROUGH CAN BE EDUCATIONAL - YOU NEVER KNOW WHICH EXPERIENCES GOD MAY CHOOSE TO USE. TALK TO GOD ABOUT HOW WORTHWHILE YOU SEE YOUR PRESENT EDUCATION, TRAINING, JOB OR TIME OF UNEMPLOYMENT. OFFER IT TO HIM TO USE, IF YOU MEAN BUSINESS. DON'T BE IMPATIENT IF GOD DOESN'T SEEM TO BE USING YOU FOR VERY MUCH RIGHT NOW. SPEAK TO HIM, ASK HIM TO SHOW YOU WHAT HE WANTS FROM YOUR LIFE. (HE MAY ONLY WANT TO REVEAL THE NEXT CHAPTER, RATHER THAN THE WHOLE LIFE STORY!)

EXODUS 3:1-17

DO YOU EVER FEEL LIKE YOU ARE A NOBODY, SO GOD WOULDN'T BE INTERESTED IN YOUR LIFE? WELL, YOU ARE NOT ALONE. MOST PEOPLE FEEL LIKE THAT AT SOME POINT IN THEIR LIFE. EVEN MOSES DID (V 11).

YOU ARE NOT ALONE.

Do any of these sentences apply to you?

• Sometimes I feel really useless.
• God expects too much from me.
• Often I know what I ought to do, but haven't a clue where to start.
• Even if I did try to be braver as a Christian, I don't suppose anyone would notice.
• I'm bigger than I think I am, because I know for sure God is on my side.

The more that applied to you – the more you're like Moses!

Check out the stories of other Bible characters who thought they were useless nobodies, and remember what they all achieved for God.

• Isaiah (Isaiah 6:5-8).
• Jeremiah (Jeremiah 1:4-10).
• Paul (1 Corinthians 15:9,10).

'I am who I am' (v 14). (One possible meaning is 'I'll always be what I want to be'.) God tells Moses to get things back into perspective. God is bigger than Moses' feeling of inferiority. With God, Moses could do the impossible. Notice 'I have decided ... I will bring them out ... and will take them!' No question with God!

How does that make you feel about your list above?

ACTION

• SPEND SOME TIME IN PRAYER ASKING GOD TO HELP YOU TRUST HIS JUDGMENT. IF YOU HAVE A LOW OPINION OF YOURSELF, TALK TO GOD ABOUT IT. GOD USES PEOPLE WHO ARE WILLING TO BE USED. IT DOESN'T MATTER HOW INTELLIGENT THEY ARE OR HOW ATTRACTIVE PEOPLE FIND THEM. TRUST THAT GOD KNOWS THE BEST PLAN FOR YOU.

EXODUS 4:1-20

THE SOURCE OF POWER
• STICKS TURN INTO SNAKES!
• A HAND BECOMES COVERED IN LEPROSY AND THEN WELL AGAIN!
• WATER TURNS INTO BLOOD!

GOD WAS SHOWING MOSES THAT, IF THE EGYPTIANS BELIEVED MAGIC TRICKS MEANT AUTHORITY, THEN HE COULD DO THE BEST TRICKS OF ALL. COME ON, MOSES! BE CONFIDENT! GOD WOULD BE THE SOURCE OF MOSES' POWER AND EVERYONE WOULD KNOW IT. BUT ...

'Please send someone else!' (v 13)

How to be rude to God in one easy lesson by Moses! Result: God gets angry, Moses gets on his donkey fast! Just another sign that no one stands in the way of God's plan.

God will give you the power to speak for him, but you may need to:
• tell him the doubts you have about your own ability (v 10)
• get someone else to help you (vs 14,15)
• work out in advance what you are going to say about God (vs 15,16).

Are you going to let God's power work in you, or run the risk of displeasing him?

ACTION

• LISTEN TO A WORSHIP SONG. SPEND SOME TIME THANKING GOD THAT HE IS SO POWERFUL AND THAT NOTHING IS BEYOND HIS CAPABILITIES.

• 'THE SAME POWER THAT BROUGHT CHRIST BACK FROM THE DEAD IS OPERATIVE WITHIN THOSE WHO ARE CHRIST'S.' LEON MORRIS.

EXODUS 4:27-5:9

'WE'RE IN THIS TOGETHER!'
MOSES WAS MUCH MORE CONFIDENT WITH AARON BESIDE HIM. TOGETHER THEY FACED THE KING OF EGYPT. BUT ...

GOOD EXCUSES.

'Who is the Lord?'
'Why should I listen to him?'
The king wasn't going to take notice of commands that came out of the sky!

People still rebel against what God says. Romans 7:7-10 shows how people often object to God because it looks as if he is making demands on them.

They may find good excuses. It wasn't unreasonable of Moses and Aaron to ask to be allowed to hold a festival to honour God. Egypt was a land of many different gods, all with their own rituals. But the king wanted to show that his own gods were superior – and anyway he was too much of a materialist (vs 4,5)!

Make a list of the people you know who aren't interested in Christianity. Can you get to the bottom of why these people won't take notice of God? Be understanding!

ACTION

• DO YOU HAVE ANY FRIENDS OR FAMILY WHO KNOW ALL ABOUT WHAT GOD SAYS BUT REFUSE TO LET IT MAKE A DIFFERENCE TO THEM? SPEND SOME TIME PRAYING FOR THEM NOW. YOU MAY FIND IT EASIER TO FOCUS IF YOU WRITE THEIR NAMES DOWN. ASK GOD TO WORK IN THEIR LIVES.

• CHECK OUT *DAYZD: EVANGELISM.*

DAYZD 23

CHECK OUT

EXODUS 5:10-6:1

DAYZD
TWENTY FOUR 24

THE KING'S PLAN WAS TO DRIVE A WEDGE BETWEEN MOSES AND THE ISRAELITES. IF THE KING TREATED THEM MORE HARSHLY, THE PEOPLE WOULD BLAME MOSES. DIVISION WEAKENS. THE KING'S PLAN WORKED (V 21), AND MOSES LET GOD KNOW ABOUT IT (VS 22,23)!

What is the outside world doing to try to divide you and your Christian friends and leaders? Do you have differences you can't cope with?

• musical taste
• fashion style
• money priorities
• Miraculous spiritual gifts or other theological issues
• groups of non-Christian friends
• political allegiance
• other

Of course, it's not wrong to have different tastes from other Christians, but do they make you hate or blame each other? If they do – then that's not on! Talk to God about it and get things sorted out.

ACTION

• EITHER BY YOURSELF OR IF YOU PRAY WITH OTHER CHRISTIANS IN A PRAYER TRIPLET, ETC, GET TOGETHER AND PRAY FOR YOUR CHURCH. ASK GOD TO PROTECT YOUR LEADERS FROM SATAN'S ATTEMPTS TO DESTROY HIS PLANS.

DAYZD 24

CHECK OUT
EXODUS 6:2-13, 7:1-7

THE ISRAELITES ARE BROKEN, HUMILIATED AND
APATHETIC. MOSES IS DISCOURAGED AND HAS HAD
ENOUGH. BUT GOD SAYS ...
'LOOK, I HAVEN'T FORGOTTEN! WHAT I HAVE SAID WILL
COME TRUE. I'M IN CHARGE AROUND HERE!'

I'M IN CHARGE AROUND HERE!

For the first time in the Bible the word save is used here (6:6) to suggest God getting the people back to where they ought to be. Moses should tell the king that the Israelites would be leaving for good (v 13).

When Jesus said, 'It is finished!' (John 19:30), he was talking about the same work that was going on here in Egypt, the work of saving God's people.

Think about your own relationship with God. Do you believe that he has rescued you? It may not mean that you have been necessarily rescued from a place. God rescues all his believers from sin and his plan is for all Christians to spend eternity with him. Give thanks to God for rescuing you.

ACTION

• CHECK OUT EPHESIANS 1:10 FOR A SUMMARY OF ALL THAT GOD WANTS FOR HIS PEOPLE. PICK ANY VERSE IN TODAY'S READING THAT HAS A HINT OF THAT IDEA.

DAYZD 25

EXODUS 11:1-12:14

THE FINAL STRAW!
• STERN WARNING TO PHARAOH (11:4-8). MOSES GAVE HIM GOD'S MESSAGE. THIS IS THE LAST PLAGUE. YOU HAVE BEEN WARNED!

• STRICT INSTRUCTIONS TO THE ISRAELITES (12:1-14). THIS IS A FESTIVAL YOU WILL KEEP FOR EVER (V 14). GOD WANTS YOU TO DO IT RIGHT.

The Passover gains extra significance for all Christians because Jesus died at Passover time:

Old celebration
• All Jews celebrate the Passover.
• They remember the time when they were rescued by God from slavery in Egypt.
• On that first Passover, the Israelites killed a male lamb or goat without any defects and smeared its blood on the door-post. God's angel killed all the eldest sons in the Egyptians' families, but 'passed over' the Israelites' houses.

New meaning
Jesus' death means:
• Everyone can become part of God's Kingdom.
• Freedom from having to do wrong – the slavery of sin.
• Eating bread and drinking wine remind us of Jesus' sacrifice as the sinless Lamb of God (Mark 14:22,23). God will now 'pass over' his people and will not punish them for their sins (Mark 14:24).

ACTION

• CHECK OUT THE WORDS FROM THIS SONG 'YOU HAVE RESCUED ME', JONNY BAKER.

YOU HAVE RESCUED ME
GIVEN ME JOY AND SET ME FREE
RESTORED MY HUMANITY
YOU HAVE RESCUED ME.

I LACKED PURPOSE, DIRECTION AND MEANING,
COULDN'T MAKE SENSE OF LIVING IN THIS WORLD
EACH WAY I TURNED THERE SEEMED NO SOLUTION
THEN YOU CAME AND RESCUED ME.

MY HEART WAS SELFISH, PROUD AND DECEITFUL,
THOUGH I TRIED I COULDN'T SEEM TO CHANGE
TRAPPED IN MY SIN AND DISILLUSIONED
THEN YOU CAME AND RESCUED ME.

YOUR IMAGE IN ME WAS TWISTED AND BROKEN,
BUT YOU HAVE BEGUN TO MAKE ME NEW
IN YOUR PLAN TO FREE THE CREATION
THANKS THAT YOU INCLUDED ME.

EXODUS 12:21-36

FREEDOM

'FREEDOM IS THE EXCHANGING OF ONE SORT OF SLAVERY FOR ANOTHER.' DO YOU THINK THE ISRAELITES WOULD HAVE FELT LIKE THAT AS THEY LEFT EGYPT AFTER YEARS OF SLAVERY?

BUT WOULD THEY HAVE BEEN AS SURE AS MOSES THAT THIS WAS A GOOD MOVE (SEE HEBREWS 11:27,28)?

Do you know any new Christians? They may have mixed feelings about the step they have just taken. We say that real freedom is believing in Jesus, but being a Christian means having your whole life-style changed and meeting God's demands. Freedom doesn't come easily.

Use these verses to get a biblical picture of freedom:
• Proverbs 29:6,
• Ezekiel 37:23,
• John 8:33-36,
• Galatians 5:1,13-15,
• Hebrews 10:19,20.

ACTION

• TRY TO MAKE TIME TO HELP ANY NEW CHRISTIANS YOU KNOW WHO MAY BE HAVING SECOND THOUGHTS. ASSURE THEM THAT THEY HAVE NOT JUST EXCHANGED ONE SORT OF SLAVERY FOR ANOTHER.

• READ A STORY ABOUT SOMEONE FROM PRESENT DAY WHO HAS BEEN HELD CAPTIVE, EG SOME OTHER RAINBOW, JOHN McCARTHY. WHAT WERE THE DIFFICULTIES THEY HAD IN ADAPTING TO LIFE AFTER CAPTIVITY?

CHECK OUT

EXODUS 13:20-22, 14:5-31

Sheer panic (14:10-12), then God uses:

• Moses (14:13)
• a strong east wind (14:21)
• the pillar of fire and cloud (v 24)
• the soft sand (v 25)
• the night (v 27)
• the torrential rain, thunder and lightning (Psalm 77:16-20)
in a build-up of natural and supernatural events to combat a powerful and well-organised army and give the victory to an ill-equipped and terrified travelling community. Here is the rescue of the Israelites, and judgment on the Egyptians.

NOTHING CAN STOP GOD'S PLANS!

Dead bodies on the shore. As the Israelites looked back, the Egyptian bodies must have been a clear sign that they were free. Similarly in baptism Christians look back at their old life and forward to the new life ahead (Romans 6:2-4).

Nothing can stop God's plans!

In one prayer, combine thanksgiving to God for the way he used power to save the Israelites and for the way he is destroying wrong in you.

ACTION

• ARE THERE THINGS WHICH YOU FIND HARD TO LEAVE BEHIND FROM YOUR NON-CHRISTIAN LIFE? ASK GOD TO HELP YOU DEAL WITH THOSE THINGS. WRITE THEM DOWN ON TO A PIECE OF PAPER OR IN A PRAYER DIARY. PRAY THROUGH EACH ITEM AND THEN WHEN YOU HAVE FINISHED, RIP THE PAGE/PIECE OF PAPER OUT/UP AND THROW IT AWAY. ASK GOD TO DO THE SAME WITH YOUR SINS.

EXODUS 16:1-21

MOAN, MOAN, MOAN.
IMAGINE THE BORED CONVERSATION (VS 3,4):

Israelite 1: Of course, it's not like it used to be in Egypt, is it?
Israelite 2: No ... no, it's not.
Israelite 1: We were prisoners then, of course ... but at least we had enough to eat.
Israelite 2: That's right, yeah.
Israelite 1: No ... that Moses couldn't organise an exodus if he tried, could he?
Israelite 2: And he expects us to believe food is going to fall out of the sky. Ha! Of course it won't, will it? ... no.
Moses: God is really the one who is organising this, so don't be so sure about the food !

(Read 15:27 and 16:1 together to see another reason for their moaning. Maybe they'd had it too good at Elim!)

Result: God appeared to them in a dazzling light (vs 7,10), and they had as much manna and quail (a luxury!) as they could eat (v 18).

The people had nothing else to complain about. But even so, some of them just couldn't keep the rules (v 20).

Which of these statements can you relate to:

• Things have never been so bad.
• I'm not sure my church/group leader knows what he's doing.
• I want what God has to offer, but I try to bend his rules.
• I wish God would prove himself more.

ACTION

• ACCORDING TO TODAY'S VERSES, WHICH IS THE LESSON YOU MOST NEED TO LEARN?

• IF GOD HAS BROUGHT US OUT OF THE CAPTIVITY OF SIN, SURELY HE IS GOING TO KEEP ON PROVIDING FOR OUR NEEDS? PRAY THAT YOU WILL TRUST GOD TO GUIDE AND PROVIDE THE THINGS THAT YOU NEED IN YOUR LIFE.

EXODUS 19:1-25

MET BY GOD

WHO SAID BEING IN TOUCH WITH GOD ISN'T EXCITING AND DEMANDING! WHICH VERSES RELATE TO THESE SENTENCES?

EXCITING AND DEMANDING!

- Moses meets God.
- God: You and the people are mine. I chose you.
- People: We'll do anything you say, Lord.
- God: Watch out for the cloud. That will be me.
- Get ready. Get washed.
- Don't have sex.
- Thunder, lightning, the cloud and a trumpet.
- The people meet God.
- God: Keep your distance! But let Aaron through.

God is:

- A loving Father (v 5),
- The Creator of high standards in life-style (vs 10,11),
- A powerful Lord (v 18).

ACTION

• ASK GOD TO HELP YOU NOT TO LIMIT HIM BY YOUR OWN INTELLECTUAL ABILITIES. WE OFTEN ONLY SEE GOD IN A ONE-DIMENSIONAL ROLE, EG AS A LOVING FATHER. TRY NOW TO RELATE TO HIM ON THESE THREE DIFFERENT LEVELS. SPEND TIME REALISING THE CLAIM HE HAS ON YOUR LIFE BECAUSE HE HAS THESE THREE ROLES.

EXODUS 20:1-21

GOD HAS GIVEN US GUIDELINES TO LIVE BY. COMMANDMENTS MEAN WORDS. (CHECK EXODUS 34:28.) THEY ARE GENERAL PRINCIPLES FOR THE ISRAELITES ON WHICH TO HANG ALL THE SPECIFIC LAWS.

Note: The main reasons for keeping the commandments are humankind's special relationship with God (v 2) and our response to God's love (v 6). Pretending to love God won't work (vs 3-7).

GUIDELINES TO LIVE BY.

The Ten Commandments are all about what we can't do. Doesn't that make Christianity a bit dull?

People often criticise the Ten Commandments for being very restrictive – all those 'Do not's'. But it would have been far more restrictive if God had actually spelt out what we should do. Suppose God had given us positive commandments:

• You should discover a cure for the common cold.
• Write an orchestral symphony.
• You should design a toilet which doesn't need water to flush it.
• You should develop the technology to sustain life on Mars.

But instead of giving us endless lists and telling us what to do, he has simply left us to discover, to wonder, to make theories, to invent for ourselves.

ACTION

• TALK TO GOD ABOUT WHAT YOU THINK ABOUT HIS GUIDELINES FOR LIVING. ARE THERE THINGS IN YOUR LIFE WHICH ANGER GOD? WRITE A LIST OF TEN THINGS WHICH YOU WANT TO DO TO IMPROVE YOUR RELATIONSHIP WITH GOD, EG I WANT TO SPEND MORE TIME WITH HIM. ONLY WRITE DOWN THE THINGS THAT YOU REALLY WANT TO DO.

EXODUS 24:1-18

TO BE GUIDED BY GOD WE NEED TO BE CLOSE TO GOD.

WITH A BUSINESS CONTRACT NEITHER PARTNER HAS THE SLIGHTEST PERSONAL INTEREST IN THE OTHER. THEY OFTEN NEVER MEET FACE TO FACE.

God's contract with his people is different:

• God wants them to get it right about his commands. The whole agreement is based on making promises (v 3), on written unchanging guidelines (v 12), on lavish purification ceremonies to show that everyone is serious (v 8).

FACE TO FACE.

• Aaron, Moses, his sons Nadab and Abihu (and seventy leaders of Israel) have the closest possible contact with God, a unique experience of him vs 9-11).

Is your relationship with God ...
• Based on mutual commitment. He is 100 per cent committed to you. How much do you give back?
• One where you understand the privilege of being close to him (with the result that you too can see the dazzling light of God's presence, v 16, 2 Corinthians 3:18).

Remember: Commitment could cost you everything!

ACTION

• SPEND SOME TIME IN PRAYER. ASK GOD TO FORGIVE YOU FOR THE TIMES WHEN YOUR RELATIONSHIP WITH HIM IS ONE-SIDED. ASK HIM TO HELP YOU BE MORE COMMITTED TO KNOWING HIM.

EXODUS 32:1-21

BETRAYAL OF THE TRUTH

THE ISRAELITES WEREN'T CHOSEN BY GOD FOR ANY GOOD QUALITIES THEY HAD. THAT'S OBVIOUS! THEY HAD BEEN AFRAID AND HAD COMPLAINED BITTERLY AS THEY JOURNEYED THROUGH THE WILDERNESS, AND NOW, WORST OF ALL, THEY REBELLED AGAINST HIM, OPENLY AND OBSCENELY (V 6). LATER STEPHEN WAS ASHAMED OF HIS PREDECESSORS BECAUSE OF IT (ACTS 7:38-41). ON DAY ONE THEY BROKE RULE ONE.

THEY BROKE RULE ONE.

Israel
deserved to be
totally rejected by God –
he could just as well kill them
and start all over again (v 10)!

Then God saw Moses' commitment to
the agreement (v 13), and changed his
mind about killing the people.

How are you going to make sure you don't
betray the truth and harm your relationship
with God?

Here are a few suggestions:

• Don't let any short-term 'high'
experiences be a God-substitute (vs 4,6).
• Remember: your relationship with him
doesn't depend on how well you
perform, but on his love that never
gives up on you (1 John 3:19-24).
Take notice of your
conscience and relax!

ACTION

• SPEND SOME TIME IN PRAYER AND MEDITATION. THIS PASSAGE SHOWS A PEOPLE WHICH GOD HAS RESCUED AND GUIDED AWAY FROM SLAVERY, NOT BEING GRATEFUL FOR WHAT GOD HAS DONE BUT WORSHIPPING ANOTHER GOD. HOW QUICKLY THEY FORGOT WHAT GOD HAD DONE FOR THEM. DO YOU FIND YOURSELF DRIFTING AWAY FROM GOD WHEN THE GOING GETS TOUGH OR WHEN HE HASN'T GIVEN YOU WANT YOU WANT?

EXODUS 32:30-33:6

DAYZD 34

NO TAME GOD!

WHEN PEOPLE DESCRIBE GOD THEY USUALLY USE WORDS LIKE: LOVING, POWERFUL, KIND, ETERNAL, FAIR, CREATOR, FATHER, SAVIOUR ...

What about these words: angry, punitive, judge, destructive. Do they describe the God that you know? If you don't think so read through the passage again.

Not very cosy! No faith and no obedience means no relationship with God and in the end that will make people miserable (33:3,4).

Help! People won't get away with rebelling against God for ever. No one automatically goes to heaven. For everyone who will die today in the world, this is their last chance to put things right with him. After that, all those unpleasant descriptions of God could come into play.

GOD IS ...

What features of Moses' character stand out in this passage. How can you learn from him?

ACTION

• READ CAREFULLY AND SLOWLY HEBREWS 10:26-31 AND TAKE SIN IN YOUR OWN LIFE AND OTHER PEOPLE'S REBELLION AGAINST GOD SERIOUSLY! BUT IF YOU FEEL SUICIDAL, HAVE A SNEAK PREVIEW OF TOMORROW'S VERSES!

DAYZD 34

EXODUS 33:12-34:9

STILL MY PEOPLE

MOSES ASKS FOR SIGNS THAT GOD WILL STILL BE WITH THEM (VS 16,18), AND GOD RESPONDS. WHAT AN AMAZING WAY GOD GUIDED HIS PEOPLE!

GOD RESPONDS.

He loves Moses and the people so much that:
• he will give them victory over their enemies (33:14),
• he gives Moses a private glimpse of himself (33:22,23, 34:5),
• he gives them a second chance with the stone tablets (34:1).

In your own Christian life have you recently:
• made any new breakthroughs in getting things right?
• seen another side to God?
• understood what it means to be forgiven and to have a second chance? If so, that's God's love at work! Thank him. He's helping you be distinctive (33:16).

Did you know that Christ's light in us can be a beacon to other people to come to know him? How did you become a Christian? Many people become Christians through friends. Was it the light in their life which attracted you to God?

• CHECK OUT THE 34:34,35. WHAT AN AMAZING COUPLE OF VERSES! TRY TO IMAGINE THE RADIANCE IN MOSES' FACE AFTER MEETING WITH GOD. DO YOU FEEL RADIANT AFTER MEETING WITH GOD. CHECK OUT 2 CORINTHIANS 3:18 AND LUKE 11:36. CAN PEOPLE TELL FROM SEEING YOU THAT YOU HAVE BEEN IN THE PRESENCE OF GOD? ASK GOD TO HELP YOU BE A LIGHT IN THIS WORLD.

'IF CHRIST IS WITH US, WHO IS AGAINST US? YOU CAN FIGHT WITH CONFIDENCE WHERE YOU ARE SURE OF VICTORY. WITH CHRIST AND FOR CHRIST VICTORY IS CERTAIN.' *SAINT BERNARD OF CLAIRVAUX.*

DAYZD 35

EXODUS 35:1-9, 20-29

DULL AND INSIGNIFICANT.

'WORK HARD FOR GOD! BE GENEROUS!' SAYS MOSES AS THE WHOLE ISRAELITE COMMUNITY STARTS TO CONSTRUCT THE SHRINE THAT WAS DESIGNED BY GOD HIMSELF. IT MEANS THE PEOPLE MUST:

• Use the Sabbath properly – part of the covenant agreement with God, (vs 1-3). How is your 'rest day' different from every other day in your week? What makes it God-centred?
• Give what they want to (vs 20,21). Even those not in work or without a skill give personal jewellery or raw materials for the shrine. When was the last time you said, 'Nothing I've got is any use to God'? Everyone has something to offer.

Look at Romans 12, and add up the number of verses that demand hard work and generosity from a Christian.

Offer something new to God now, if you want to. Then make sure you commit yourself to giving it today.

ACTION

• CHECK OUT 1 CORINTHIANS 15:58. IT IS ENCOURAGING TO KNOW THAT EVEN WHEN WE ARE NOT SURE HOW GOD IS GUIDING AND USING US HE IS. THINK ABOUT EVENTS IN YOUR OWN LIFE. IT'S HARD TO IMAGINE HOW GOD USES THE DULL AND INSIGNIFICANT THINGS TO HIS GLORY. THANK HIM THAT EVEN THOUGH THERE ARE THINGS IN OUR LIVES THAT WE DON'T RATE VERY HIGHLY, HE IS STILL USING THEM FOR HIS GOOD.

EXODUS 39:32-43, 40:34-38

MOSES APPROVES (39:32,42,43), AND GOD MOVES IN (40:34). IN FACT, GOD IS THERE SO MUCH THAT EVEN MOSES, HIS FAITHFUL SERVANT, HAS TO KEEP OUT (40:35)! (NOW CAN YOU UNDERSTAND THE SIGNIFICANCE OF HEBREWS 10:19-25? READ IT NOW.)

DECISIONS.

God's promise is kept (see 29:45) – he is living with his people. They are filled with hope and confidence about what lies ahead. But the tent was just a sign that God was with them, the wind and fire (40:38) signs that he was leading them to the land he had promised.

Challenge: A non-Christian asks you, 'How do you know God is living with you? And what makes you so confident that your future is all under control?' In the absence of dazzling lights, clouds and fire, how would you answer?

After you have thought of an appropriate answer, commit it to God. If you can't think of an answer, ask God to help you out. The most important thing to remember is to be honest – both with God and with the people who ask you. There are going to be times when you feel God is far away and your life is completely out of control, but still we have to trust that God is working behind the scenes.

ACTION

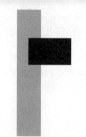

• RE-READ 40:34-38. WHEREVER YOU ARE READING THIS NOW, IMAGINE THAT YOU ARE SURROUNDED BY THE PRESENCE OF GOD. WHAT ARE THE SIGNS YOU HAVE WHICH TELL YOU GOD IS AROUND? WHATEVER DECISIONS YOU ARE HAVING TO MAKE THIS WEEK, BIG OR SMALL, ASK GOD TO BE THERE WITH YOU AND GUIDE YOU.

NUMBERS 9:15-23

FOLLOW GOD.

IT WAS EASY FOR THE ISRAELITES TO KNOW WHAT GOD WAS TELLING THEM. THEY HAD GOD'S CLOUD TO GUIDE THEM DAY AND NIGHT.

YOU DON'T KNOW WHETHER TO GO TO COLLEGE/UNIVERSITY OR NOT. WHAT SORT OF GUIDANCE DO YOU LOOK FOR? YOU COULD JUST SIT AND STARE BLANKLY AT THE WALL, WAITING FOR SOME SUPERNATURAL KICK UP THE PANTS. AND GOD MAY DO THAT! BUT MORE OFTEN, GOD'S GUIDANCE IS ALL ROUND YOU ANYWAY:

STARE BLANKLY AT THE WALL.

1. Have you got good enough qualifications?
2. What do those who care most for you think?
3. Does it make sense financially?
4. Do you know anything in the Bible that shows that your motive for wanting to go is wrong?
5. Why not apply anyway? A rejection may mean apply somewhere else, the time isn't right to go or as far as God is concerned, college is not for you.
6. Be honest with God about it, and say you want to do what pleases him.

But do something! Don't just sit there! Are you looking for clouds and fire, when God wants you to use your mind, eyes, ears and the tongue in your head?

ACTION

• CHECK OUT PHIL JENSON'S BOOK *THE LAST WORD ON GUIDANCE* PUBLISHED BY ST MATTHIAS PRESS AS AN EXTRA RESOURCE.

NUMBERS 13:1,2, 17-33

NEXT STOP - PROMISED LAND!

IMAGINE CALEB THE SPY WRITING A POSTCARD TO THE REST OF THE ISRAELITES AFTER VERSE 24.

To: Moses and Co,
The Wilderness, Somewhere between Egypt and Palestine.

Dear All,
Great place! God was right. It's as if it's flowing with milk and honey! Grapes, pomegranates, figs – you name it! One or two big guys around though. Having a fantastic time. Back soon. Wish you were all here.
Love, Caleb.

THE SPY WRITING A POSTCARD.

The people were divided in their reaction. Some had faith (v 30), but they were in the minority. The others were afraid (v 31) and didn't want to know.

When your church makes new plans, there is often the same division – the 'let's keep things as they are' crowd and the 'step of faith and believe it will happen' crowd. Who is right may not be as clear as it is in today's verses.

ACTION

• PRAY THROUGH THE ARGUMENTS FOR AND AGAINST MAKING CHANGE IN YOUR CHURCH OR YOUTH GROUP. ASK GOD TO GUIDE THOSE WHO NEED TO MAKE THE DECISIONS AND PRAY THAT THEY WILL HAVE WISDOM IN ALL THEIR DECISION-MAKING.

NUMBERS 14:1-25

MOAN, MOAN, MOAN . . .

'PAH! IT WAS BETTER IN EGYPT. HEAPS OF FOOD. PEACE AND QUIET. AH, THE GOOD OLD DAYS. RECKON WE'D DO BETTER TO GO BACK THERE.'

THERE'S NO PLEASING SOME PEOPLE. GOD GOT ANGRY AND NONE OF THOSE WHO COMPLAINED WERE ALLOWED INTO THE PROMISED LAND. FORTY YEARS OF WALKING FOR NOTHING EXCEPT THE KNOWLEDGE THAT THEIR DESCENDANTS WOULD BENEFIT. GOD COULD ONLY STAND SO MUCH MOANING, BECAUSE IT SHOWED HOW LITTLE FAITH THE PEOPLE HAD.

THERE'S NO PLEASING SOME PEOPLE.

Check out as many of these verses as possible to see what the Bible says about moaning.

• Job 23:1-17, 42:2-6
• Philippians 2:14,15
• Colossians 3:13

To doubt God is something we all have to go through.

Spend some time in prayer asking God to help you get through the doubting times.

ACTION

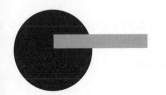

• 'THE ART OF DOUBTING IS EASY, FOR IT IS AN ABILITY THAT IS BORN WITH US.' MARTIN LUTHER.

JOSHUA 1:1-18

HOW TO BE SUCCESSFUL

GOD GIVES JOSHUA A BOOST OF FAITH RIGHT WHEN HE
NEEDS IT. JOSHUA WAS PROBABLY NERVOUS BECAUSE:

A BOOST

OF FAITH!

• he was now responsible for all the people (v 6),
• the future was in his hands (vs 3,4),
• Moses was a difficult act to follow (v 2).

God gives him the best possible help. 'I will
always be with you' (v 5), and that's final!

But Joshua's success is conditional. What were
the conditions? Check out verses 7 and 8.

Does this mean that we don't have to look for a
minute-by-minute, supernatural guidance if we
are responding positively to the Bible?

Flick back through the last few *DAYZD* notes, and
pray about the new understanding you have of
what it means to:

• be part of God's people,
• enjoy freedom,
• have a sense of direction,
• know God is with you always.

ACTION

• A HELPFUL WAY TO REMEMBER THAT GOD DOES GUIDE US IS BY
KEEPING A PRAYER DIARY. KEEP A RECORD OF ALL THAT YOU PRAY
ABOUT OVER THE COMING MONTHS. LEAVE A SPACE SO THAT AS GOD
ANSWERS YOUR PRAYERS YOU CAN WRITE DOWN WHAT HAPPENED.

GENESIS 24:1-27

DAY-D
FORTY
TWO
42

ANOTHER WAY TO BE GUIDED BY GOD IS TO LISTEN TO WHAT HE HAS TO SAY. THE NEXT EIGHTEEN STUDIES FOCUS ON TIMES WHEN GOD SPOKE TO HIS PEOPLE. BEFORE YOU START THIS SECTION, SPEND SOME TIME IN PRAYER. ASK GOD TO HELP YOU LISTEN TO EVERYTHING HE HAS TO SAY TO YOU.

LISTEN TO WHAT HE HAS TO SAY.

An unusual way to find a marriage-partner!

Abraham's servant can teach us about listening to God, when we need him to guide us in making decisions.

1. He prayed (vs 12-14). It's okay to ask for a definite 'sign' like this, if you need it. God doesn't guarantee to give it, but often he does, as here (vs 17-19).
2. He watched (v 21). He stayed open to God. Many people ask for God's guidance, but then switch the 'receiver' off.
3. He praised (vs 26,27). When God clearly spoke, he heard, and he stopped to say thanks.

What questions do you need God to answer? Keep listening!

ACTION

• WRITE OUT PROVERBS 3:6, AND CARRY IT WITH YOU TODAY, WHERE YOU WILL KEEP SEEING IT.

DAY-D 42

MOST OF US FIND IT HARD TO KNOW WHAT GOD'S WILL IS FOR US. OVER THE NEXT TWO DAYS WE ARE GOING TO BE LOOKING AT WAYS WE CAN SEEK GOD'S GUIDANCE.

Read this fascinating story of an ordinary young woman who was seeking God's guidance in what turned out to be an extraordinary life:

Jackie Pullinger wanted to be a missionary. An ex-student of the Royal College of Music, she was too young and unqualified to be accepted by some of the missionary societies to which she applied, while others did not want musicians; but she still felt drawn by God into missionary work. 'Trust me, and I will lead you,' God had said.

Following the advice of an Anglican minister, she just went; she took a one-way ticket to China and disembarked from the boat at Hong Kong around the time that the cultural revolution was starting in China. She found a part-time teaching job at a mission school in the Walled City, and played the harmonium at the Sunday services. Not much, she felt, but it was a start.

 When Jackie arrived in 1966 her first move was to open a youth club for the Walled City's teenage gang members; and she did more – she also helped them find jobs, went with them to court and became involved in helping families.

When news of her willingness spread, other people in the city began to approach her as well. They assumed that as a Westerner she could get anything for them, and while she was unable to meet many of their demands, she was prepared to be used in this way. Her hope was that by 'walking the extra mile' she might be able to show them something about Jesus.

But the club seemed a failure and her attempts to speak about Jesus met with blank stares, or a nod and a 'Yeah, yeah, that's nice.' She was further troubled by the attitude of some of the more established missionaries on the Island, who no longer appeared to expect to see anyone won to Christ.

Encouraged by two Chinese Christians, Jackie experienced a baptism of the Holy Spirit and received the gift of speaking in tongues. There was nothing emotional about it, and it was six weeks before she began to notice that something remarkable was happening – now that she had let God have a hand in her prayers, Chinese youngsters began coming to Christ.

To provide for the new converts, Jackie started a Bible study at the Mission and on Sundays took them along to the evening service. The congregation, however, did not take too kindly to these unkempt young people, so on the advice of an old missionary she started her own worship services on a Sunday morning. Later she began a Saturday evening prayer meeting which attracted a wide range of Christians and proved to be the 'power house' behind her ministry.

Much of her outreach was directed towards the Triad gangs who controlled life in the Walled City. These secret societies has originally been formed in the seventeenth century to overthrow the Manchu dynasty; today they are criminal gangs who make money by controlling gambling and opium dens. Jackie's first contact with a Triad gang came the night after her youth club had been broken into and vandalised and the 14K Triad leader, Goko, sent his 'fighter-fixer' – to guard the club against further trouble.

Jackie's mission is not only to the Triads; she works among the poor and the destitute, street sleepers, prostitutes and drug addicts. She looks for the 'poor in spirit and body', to show them that they are loved and can find new life and hope. Most of them are addicts and she has led many of them to Christ.

Over the years God has wonderfully provided for the work and Jackie has at times been amazed to see how income has grown as her 'family' increased; gifts of money and in kind have arrived, often anonymously. Asked one day by a persistent questioner, 'Where does your money come from?' they were both startled when someone knocked at the door bearing an envelope for Jackie which contained a hundred dollar bill. The questioner was suitably impressed!

(Extract taken from *70 Great Christians Changing the World,* Geoffrey Hanks, © Christian Focus Publishing. Used by permission.)

1.
• Jackie knew God was guiding her by 'pushing doors'. Are there any areas where you are seeking guidance? What can you do to find out what God's will is for you?

• Was it easy for her when she arrived in Hong Kong? What did she do to overcome these difficulties?

2.
Three ways to find out God's guidance are:

Persistent prayer.
Regular Bible reading.
'Pushing doors'.

• Check out Matthew 7:7,8. How can these verses help when we are seeking God's guidance? Try out what the verses suggest.

• Pray now for the areas in your life in which you need God's guidance. Ask him to show you the right thing to do. Ask him to give you his wisdom and insight when trying to find the right solution.

• Don't give in. Keep communicating with God until you know what the answer is. Be patient and listen to your conscience.

1 SAMUEL 3:1-10

GOD EVIDENTLY SPOKE OUT LOUD. HAVE YOU EVER HEARD HIM DO THIS? IT SEEMS IT WASN'T COMMON THEN (V 1); AND IT ISN'T NOW.

HAVE YOU EVER HEARD HIM DO THIS?

Can you add to this list of ways that God often speaks to us?

• Through our consciences.
• Through his words in the Bible.
•
•

Why didn't Samuel answer God when he first called him? How did he know it was God speaking to him?

Today we can test whether it is God speaking to us by checking it out in the Bible. God never contradicts what he has said in the Bible. You could also do as Samuel did, speak to a mature Christian about it.

Take Samuel's prayer in verses 9 and 10 and pray it for yourself:

(a) for these readings on listening to God,
(b) for the rest of today.

ACTION

• SPEND A TIME IN MEDITATION AND PRAISE. ASK GOD'S SPIRIT TO SPEAK TO YOU NOW. OPEN YOUR EARS AND YOUR HEART TO WHAT GOD IS SAYING TO YOU. DON'T BE PUT OFF IF YOU DON'T HEAR STRAIGHT AWAY FROM GOD. IF YOU WANT TO TALK TO HIM HE WILL WANT TO TALK TO YOU. REMEMBER, GOD SPEAKS TO US IN MANY WAYS.

CHECK OUT

1 SAMUEL 16:1-13

HOW DID GOD 'SAY' ALL THIS TO SAMUEL?

There are clues in:

verse 4 – Samuel is a 'seer', someone with the gift of sensing the future king when he sees him;

verses 6,7 – God's way of looking at the question comes clear for Samuel as he thinks it over.

Check out Romans 8:16. Paul describes this 'inner voice' as God's Spirit communicating with our spirit to make us sure of something.

INNER VOICE.

How do we know that God had chosen David and rejected Saul? Check out 2 Corinthians 1:22 to see what that means for us today.

Think about the last sentence of verse 7; ask what it is 'saying' to you; then complete, either in your head or in your prayer diary, this sentence: God's 'inner voice' is telling me ...

ACTION

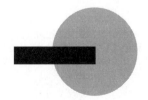

• THIS PASSAGE SHOWS US THAT GOD CHOOSES PEOPLE FOR THEIR INNER QUALITIES RATHER THAN THEIR EXTERNAL ONES. IT'S EASY TO THINK THAT ALL SUCCESSFUL PEOPLE ARE PERFECT. DO YOU SEE ANYONE ON TELEVISION HAVING A 'BAD HAIR AND SKIN DAY'?

GOD'S SUCCESS IS NOT THE SAME AS THE WORLD'S. HIS STANDARDS ARE GREATER AND HE SEES BENEATH THE SKIN. PRAY THAT YOU WILL BE MORE CONCERNED WITH WHAT YOUR HEART SAYS ABOUT YOU RATHER THAN WITH YOUR BODY.

PROVERBS 4

CROSS OUT THE INCORRECT
DEDUCTIONS FROM VERSE 7:

WISDOM IS ...
UNNECESSARY/QUITE
USEFUL/ABSOLUTELY VITAL.

WISDOM IS THE GROWING
ABILITY TO KNOW HOW GOD
WANTS US TO LIVE, EACH
HOUR OF EACH DAY. THE
WRITER MENTIONS TWO
COMMON SOURCES OF WISDOM:

EACH HOUR OF EACH DAY.

1. Parents (vs 1-9). Think of two pieces of good advice God has given you through your parents.

2. Teachers (vs 10-13). Think of two gems you have learnt from teachers at church, school or college.

How many wise commands can you count in this chapter? Which is the one you need to listen to today?

God is both our Father and a teacher. Do we listen to what he has to say to us?

• CHECK OUT VS 18,19. WHICH ROAD DO YOU THINK YOU ARE TRAVELLING ON? ASK GOD TO SHINE HIS LIGHT SO THAT YOU CAN SEE WHICH ROAD YOU SHOULD BE ON.

RUTH 3

AS WITH THE CHOICE OF REBECCA FOR ISAAC, THIS MATCH-MAKING SYSTEM MAY SEEM STRANGE TO US! IN OLD TESTAMENT TIMES:

• Marriages were arranged by parents. Ruth unquestioningly left the decisions to Naomi. (As a young widow, she lived with her mother-in-law, not her mother.)

• Widows (and others without financial support) were the responsibility of their 'closest relative' – see Leviticus 25:25. So Ruth appealed (even proposed!) to Boaz (v 9).

Read on into chapter 4, to discover how God wove this system into his purposes for his chosen people.

God can equally well help us to find a husband/wife through the twentieth-century system – provided we listen and submit to his will.

Who would you go to for advice about love and marriage?

What sort of questions would you need to ask them?

God is concerned about every aspect of our lives. Pray that when the time comes to choose a marriage partner you will make wise decisions.

MATCH-MAKING

ACTION

• CHECK OUT *DAYZD: RELATIONSHIPS* TO FIND OUT WHAT THE BIBLE SAYS ABOUT CHOOSING THE RIGHT PARTNER.

• ANOTHER GOOD RESOURCE IS *GOD, SEX, MARRIAGE*, JOHN RICHARDSON, ST MATTHIAS PRESS.

2 JOHN

READ THE *GOOD NEWS* BIBLE'S INTRODUCTION AND FOOTNOTES TO THIS LETTER.

PART OF HEARING GOD CLEARLY IS KNOWING WHO NOT TO LISTEN TO. NOT EVERY RELIGIOUS TEACHER/BOOK IS TELLING YOU THE TRUTH. AND IT'S IMPORTANT TO KNOW THE TRUTH - COUNT HOW MANY TIMES JOHN MENTIONS IT HERE.

Think about which of these teachings are true. Put a cross by the false teaching:

1. Jesus on earth was God-become-man (v 7).
2. It doesn't matter if you don't believe this.
3. If someone goes against Jesus' teaching, they're wrong (v 9).

Have you come across false teaching of this kind?

At that time, to give hospitality to a teacher meant you agreed with him (vs 10,11). This should not stop us loving people (v 6), even if we disagree with them. But we must learn to recognise false teaching.

ACTION

• ASK GOD TO HELP YOU KNOW WHAT IS FALSE TEACHING AND WHAT IS FROM HIM. CHECK OUT JOHN 10:6. PRAY THAT YOU WILL RECOGNISE GOD'S VOICE AND FOLLOW ONLY HIM.

• CHECK OUT A TAPE ON GUIDANCE WITH STEVE CHALKE IN THE *WALKING WITH JESUS* SERIES BY SCRIPTURE UNION. IT CONTAINS TWELVE SHORT PROGRAMMES WITH MUSIC, BIBLE READINGS BY DAVID SUCHET AND THOUGHTS FOR PRAYER AND ACTION.

GALATIANS 1:11-2:9

SOME PEOPLE SAY THAT PAUL CHANGED AND DISTORTED JESUS' TEACHING. SO HOW CAN WE BE SURE THAT HE IS A TRUE, RELIABLE TEACHER OF CHRISTIANITY?

1. Christians at the time agreed that he was preaching the truth (1:23). Yet, as he proves at some length, he did not learn it from any of them (1:16-22); he learnt it directly from Jesus (1:11,12).

2. The other apostles agreed that this proved he was a fellow-apostle with them (2:1,2,6-9), in no way contradicting them or dependent on them for his authority.

This means we can use the whole New Testament (the record of the apostles' teaching) to check whether what we hear elsewhere is God's truth.

If there is a part of Paul's teaching which you don't understand or disagree with, talk it over with a church leader or a mature Christian friend. When we read the Bible we have to remember that it was written in a particular cultural context.

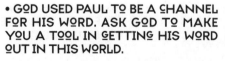

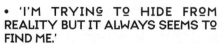

• GOD USED PAUL TO BE A CHANNEL FOR HIS WORD. ASK GOD TO MAKE YOU A TOOL IN GETTING HIS WORD OUT IN THIS WORLD.

• 'I'M TRYING TO HIDE FROM REALITY BUT IT ALWAYS SEEMS TO FIND ME.'

JONAH 1, 3:1-5

GOD GAVE JONAH A COMMAND.
JONAH THOUGHT IT WAS TOO HARD,
AND SAID NO. WE ALL DISOBEY GOD
AT TIMES; HOW HAVE YOU DONE SO
IN THE LAST WEEK?

TOO HARD?

Jonah might have expected that:

(a) God would give up on him and find someone else to go to Nineveh,
(b) He would be drowned in the stormy sea as a punishment for disobeying God,
(c) The Ninevites would laugh at him and call him a freak,
(d) The wicked Ninevites would kill him for preaching against them.

In each case, what actually happened?

Jonah tried to disobey God. God had plans for Jonah which Jonah wasn't happy with. The passage shows that even though we may try to stop God's plans he will make them happen anyway.

Ask God to help you be willing to go where he wants you to.

ACTION

• PERHAPS GOD IS GIVING YOU A SECOND CHANCE. WHAT DO YOU NEED TO DO?

2 SAMUEL 12:1-15

WHEN WE HAVE SINNED AGAINST GOD, WE OFTEN DON'T WANT TO HEAR HIM, AND CLOSE OUR EARS AGAINST HIM. HE SOMETIMES HAS TO FIND SUBTLE (AND NOT SO SUBTLE) WAYS THROUGH OUR DEFENCES.

NOT SO SUBTLE.

David's sin is summed up in verse 9. For the gory details, read chapter 11.

Nathan used a parable (much as Jesus did) to open David's ears to God's judgment, and lead him to confess, ie agree that he was guilty. When we confess, God forgives (v 13; compare 1 John 1:9); but he does not necessarily stop the consequences of our sin (vs 10-12,14).

Ask God to bring to mind any sin that you have not cleared up with him. Confess it, receive forgiveness, and ask for his strength not to repeat it.

We can't pray for God's guidance only when we want it. As Christians, God will guide us throughout our lives.

Ask God to forgive you for the times when you have closed your ears and your heart to what he has to say to you. Ask him make you willing to be guided in the way he knows best for you from now on.

ACTION

• EARLIER IN THIS BOOK WE LOOKED AT HOW GOD GUIDED HIS PEOPLE AND MOSES OUT OF SLAVERY AND INTO THE PROMISED LAND. GET HOLD OF THE WORDS OR A TAPE OF THE HYMN 'GUIDE ME O THOU GREAT REDEEMER/JEHOVAH' (YOU WILL FIND IT IN MOST HYMN BOOKS). READ THROUGH THE WORDS A FEW TIMES AND THINK ABOUT HOW THESE WORDS ARE STILL RELEVANT TO YOU TODAY.

2 CORINTHIANS 12:1-10

WHICH DO YOU FIND EASIEST TO BOAST ABOUT (YOU CAN TICK MORE THAN ONE)?

• 'Mountain-top' spiritual experience of God's presence.
• Prayers clearly answered.
• Illness suddenly healed.
• Spiritual 'banana skins' to humble you when you're proud.
• Permanent physical handicap.
• Prayer answered with a 'no'.

Paul boasts about the last three! Hunt through verses 9,10 to find his reason why; then put it into your own words:

How far have you grown towards understanding this and agreeing with it?

When the going gets tough for you as a Christian, what do you want to do? Check out Romans 5:3-5 and 1 Peter 4:14. What does Paul say that we should do?

ACTION

• SPEND SOME TIME IN PRAYER ASKING GOD TO HELP YOU TO BE STRONG IN DIFFICULT TIMES. THINK BACK TO DIFFICULT SITUATIONS WHICH YOU HAVE ALREADY FACED. HOW HAS GOD GUIDED YOU THROUGH THEM?

• TAKE SOME TIME NOW TO WORSHIP GOD.

PSALM 19:1-6

GOD 'SPEAKS' TO US THROUGH THE
UNIVERSE OF LIGHT AND DARKNESS HE HAS
CREATED (VS 1,2). NOT IN HUMAN
LANGUAGE, BUT IN TERMS WE CAN
CLEARLY UNDERSTAND (VS 3,4).

But
w h a t
does he say?
Take time today,
and again tonight, to
go outside and take a long
look at the sky. Look at the sun
that God has created (even if it's
not shining!); compare your thoughts
with verses 4-6. Note: Take care not to look
straight at the sun as it could damage your
eyesight.

What is God telling you – about himself, about yourself, about
life – through the rest of his creation? What do you want to say back
to him?

Read through this prayer by Walter Rauschenbush. If you think it is
appropriate, pray it now:

'O God, we thank you for this earth, our home; for the wide sky and the
blessed sun, for the salt sea and the running water, for the everlasting hills, and
the never-resting winds ... Grant us a heart wide open to all this beauty; and
save our souls from being so blind that we pass unseeing when even the
common thornbush is aflame with your glory.'

ACTION

• ISN'T IT AMAZING THAT WE HAVE A
GOD WHO IS NOT LIMITED BY
LANGUAGE. SPEND SOME TIME
MEDITATING ON THIS PSALM. ASK
GOD TO SPEAK TO YOU TODAY AND
GUIDE YOU IN THE AREAS WHICH
YOU ARE WORRIED ABOUT.

CHECK OUT

NEHEMIAH 8:1-12

OVER THE COURSE OF THIS BOOK WE HAVE SEEN THAT GOD CAN GUIDE US IN MANY DIFFERENT WAYS. IN THIS PASSAGE WE SEE HOW GOD CAN SPEAK TO US THROUGH THE BIBLE. BUT WE SHALL ONLY HEAR HIM IF OUR APPROACH IS RIGHT.

We need to:

• Listen (vs 1-3). Whether alone, in a group, with our family or in a congregation, we must open the book, and take its words in.

• Honour (vs 4-6). How do Ezra and the people show their respect for the God who caused the Bible to be written?

• Understand (vs 7,8). Who or what helps you to understand what God is saying through his book?

• React (vs 9-12). When God speaks, he moves our emotions, and moves us to share ourselves with others. What is he telling you to do as a result of this reading? (eg, could you suggest improvements to how your fellowship/Bible study group studies the Bible?)

ACTION

• MAKE THE EFFORT TO GET TO KNOW GOD BY READING YOUR BIBLE REGULARLY. LIKE ANY RELATIONSHIP HOW CAN YOU EXPECT TO BE CLOSE TO SOMEONE YOU HARDLY EVER SPEAK TO OR MEET?

DAYZD 55

60

EZEKIEL 12:1-16

EZEKIEL IS THE PATRON-SAINT OF DRAMA IN WORSHIP AND OUTREACH! WHEN PEOPLE WILL NO LONGER LISTEN TO HIS 'STRAIGHT TALKING', GOD TELLS HIM TO ACT OUT THE APPROACHING EXILE OF KING AND COUNTRYMEN.

God can use mime powerfully to provoke curiosity and questions (v 9) and much else besides, but clear words that speak God's message directly also have their part to play (vs 10-16).

Are there any other forms of art through which God can speak?

What did God say to you through a recent artistic performance you saw (eg concert, film, TV programme, pop song)? What have you done about it? Remember God can use lots of different ways to talk to his people.

Spend some time in prayer. Ask God to let all his people's gifts be used to build up his church.

ACTION

• IF YOU ARE INTERESTED IN DRAMA AND MIME, FIND OUT WHETHER YOUR CHURCH HAS A GROUP YOU CAN JOIN. IF IT DOESN'T AND YOU ARE STILL INTERESTED HOW ABOUT STARTING UP A GROUP YOURSELF.

THERE ARE MANY CHRISTIAN GROUPS WHICH ARE INVOLVED IN THE USE OF DRAMA IN CHURCHES. CHECK OUT THE *UK CHRISTIAN HANDBOOK* FOR NAMES AND ADDRESSES OR ASK YOUR CHURCH LEADERS.

DAYZD 56

EZEKIEL 37:1-14

HOW GOOD IS YOUR IMAGINATION? SPEND A FEW MINUTES 'IMAGINING' YOUR 'DREAM' HOLIDAY (MONEY NO OBJECT!). WHAT DOES GOD SHOW YOU ABOUT YOURSELF THROUGH THIS FANTASY?

Ezekiel had a lively, pictorial imagination. (If you have the Good News Bible illustrated version, look at the drawings of many of his pictorial prophesies.) God often spoke to him through 'visions' and word-pictures.

YOUR 'DREAM' HOLIDAY.

This vision of skulls and skeletons coming back to life points to a new, prosperous future for God's people after the national 'death' of exile. To understand the richness of the word-picture, you need to know that in Hebrew the same word means 'wind', 'breath' and 'spirit'. Read the passage again, replacing 'wind' and 'breath' with 'spirit' each time.

This chapter shows the regeneration of Israel in two parts. What part did Ezekiel have to play in this? If you are feeling spiritually dead at the moment ask God to revive you.

ACTION

• CHECK OUT JOEL 2:28. GOD'S SPIRIT CAN SPEAK TO ORDINARY PEOPLE TODAY THROUGH VISIONS AND DREAMS.

JEREMIAH 18:1-12

LIKE EZEKIEL, JEREMIAH WAS DEEPLY TUNED IN TO GOD'S THOUGHTS AND WORDS. HERE WE SEE HOW JEREMIAH UNDERSTOOD GOD'S WAYS MORE CLEARLY THROUGH THE EVERYDAY WORK OF A POTTER.

• God is like a potter, his people are his clay (v 6).

• When a piece of clay 'goes wrong', the potter changes plan and turns it into something else (v 4).

• So when the Jews disobeyed God, they could not expect his automatic goodness (vs 7-11).

GOD'S THOUGHTS AND WORDS.

Spend some time thinking about the things in your own life which you know go against what God wants for you. Thank God that even though you are not perfect he loves and uses you anyway. Ask God to change the things which damage your relationship with him.

Check out Romans 9:20,2. What does it reveal to you about God?

For Jesus, too, ordinary subjects – seeds – yeast – a flower – spoke of God. Look around your room. Is there anything God wants to say to you through something you can see or hear?

ACTION

MAKE A LIST OF THE THINGS IN YOUR LIFE WHICH DON'T PLEASE GOD. ASK HIM TO GIVE YOU THE STRENGTH TO STOP DOING THEM.

JEREMIAH 32:1-15

ANOTHER 'ORDINARY' EVENT
BRINGS A MESSAGE FROM GOD
TO JEREMIAH, WHEN HE'S UP
AGAINST IT. THE COUNTRY IS
BEING INVADED AND JEREMIAH
HIMSELF IS IN PRISON FOR
PROPHESYING THAT IT WOULD
COLLAPSE.

UP AGAINST IT ?

A fine moment to start buying property! Especially with all the legal red tape of contracts, witnesses and file copies. But God used this business transaction to show that he had a future for his people in the land, and that defeat and captivity were not his last word.

Think of something that has happened to you that is outside your control. Ask God to show you what you should learn from this.

What do Jeremiah's actions teach us about our obedience to God? Thank God that his insight is perfect and that he doesn't do anything to harm us.

Here is a helpful tip if you are having to make major decisions at the moment. It is important not to rush into making any decisions. If you have a few options, choose one of them and for a few days imagine that you have made the decision. Talk to God about it. Ask him to let you know if it is not the right decision. Try it out with all your options, each time talking it over with God and thinking about how you feel with the decision you have made. Having time to think over decisions helps you to know whether you are making the right choice.

ACTION

DAYZD 59

• FOR THE CHRISTIAN, 'EACH
THING, EACH HAPPENING, EACH
PERSON MUST BE SEEN FROM
TWO POINTS OF VIEW – *THE
EARTHLY AND THE HEAVENLY'.*
MICHEL QUOIST.

MATTHEW 1:18-25

GOD IS NOT LIMITED TO SPEAKING TO US DURING OUR WAKING HOURS. HERE HE SPEAKS TO JOSEPH IN A DREAM.

What do verses 13-23 tell us about Joseph's amazing obedience to God?

Which of these do you think are good reasons why God might sometimes want to talk to us in our sleep:

• Our mind goes on thinking (v 20) and sorting problems out.
• The rest of our body is relaxed and undisturbed.
• Our resistance to what God is wanting to say is asleep!
• Dreams can 'think about' long stretches of time in a split-second.

OUR WAKING HOURS.

Joseph evidently had several memorable dreams (see 2:13,19,22). Not everyone does; and not every dream is the voice of God. But is there anything to learn from the last dream you can remember?

Each night, as you go to sleep, commit your dreams to God.

ACTION

• SPEND SOME TIME IN PRAYER ASKING GOD TO BE IN CONTROL OF EVERY ASPECT OF YOUR LIFE, EVEN THE TIMES WHEN YOU ARE NOT IN CONTROL. IT'S IMPORTANT TO MAKE SURE THAT WHAT YOU THINK GOD IS SAYING TO YOU IS DEFINITELY FROM GOD. TEST IT OUT BY CHECKING IT AGAINST WHAT THE BIBLE TEACHES, IE IF YOU THINK GOD IS TELLING YOU TO START HAVING SEX WITH YOUR GIRLFRIEND BUT THE BIBLE MAKES IT CLEAR THAT SEX IS ONLY FOR MARRIAGE RELATIONSHIPS, THEN YOU ARE NOT HEARING FROM GOD. GOD IS NOT GOING TO CONTRADICT WHAT THE BIBLE TEACHES. IF YOU ARE STILL NOT SURE, TALK TO A MATURE CHRISTIAN ABOUT IT.

DAYZD 60

MATTHEW 2:1-12, 15-23

GOD IS NOT LIMITED TO SPEAKING TO OR THROUGH CHRISTIANS. THIS PASSAGE SHOWS PEOPLE GOD USED TO GET THE GOOD NEWS OF JESUS' BIRTH OUT INTO THE WORLD.

GOD IS NOT LIMITED.

• Visitors from the East learned about Jesus through the stars, and we learn from the visitors of his universal greatness. (This is the only time in the Bible that astrology is seen to 'work'; elsewhere it is scorned, eg Isaiah 47:13).

• Jewish law teachers knew the Messiah's birth-place from the Old Testament, and this shows us one of the ways in which the Old Testament prophecy came true.

Check out verses 15-23. Even when Jesus was an infant, he was fulfilling what was taught in the Old Testament. What does it teach you about the nature of prophecy?

When thinking about what job to look for, what order of value would you give to advice from:

• careers adviser
• job centre
• Christian friends
• friends who are not Christians
• parents
• minister or other leader at church

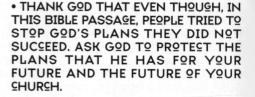

• THANK GOD THAT EVEN THOUGH, IN THIS BIBLE PASSAGE, PEOPLE TRIED TO STOP GOD'S PLANS THEY DID NOT SUCCEED. ASK GOD TO PROTECT THE PLANS THAT HE HAS FOR YOUR FUTURE AND THE FUTURE OF YOUR CHURCH.

ISAIAH 1:1-20

WE ALL TEND TO LOOK FOR IDEAL CONDITIONS AND TO BLAME OUR FAILURES ON A BAD ENVIRONMENT. VERSE 1 SETS ISAIAH IN HIS ENVIRONMENT, AGAINST THE BACKGROUND OF FOUR KINGS:

• Uzziah, a God-fearing king corrupted by pride, who ended his days in disgrace, struck down by God with a horrible disease.
• Jotham, a good king with poor judgment.
• Ahaz, a worshipper of idols.
• Hezekiah, a noble and good man, faithful to God but unable to trust and obey him in political decisions.

For God's people it was a time of internal upheaval and external threat. After the death of Solomon, the country had split into two kingdoms. Israel, the northern kingdom, had disappeared, invaded by Assyria (see 2 Kings 17:21-23). Judah, the southern kingdom, and its capital Jerusalem, were under threat from the same powerful Assyrian empire (2 Kings 18:13).

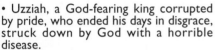

LOOK FOR IDEAL CONDITIONS.

What a time to be a prophet! Yet in the midst of all this, Isaiah hears the word of God and passes it on to the people. Verses 2–20 are his message to the nation, telling them why God has allowed them to be oppressed by their enemies.

What is the basic reason why the nation is suffering so much trouble (vs 2-4)?

Why is God rejecting the sacrifices they make to him (vs 11-17)?

What does he promise to do if they change their ways (v 18)?

What does he threaten if they continue to disobey (v 20)?

ACTION

• ASK YOURSELF: IS MY LIFE MARKED OUT BY WILLING OBEDIENCE OR SULKY REBELLION? DO I SOMETIMES TRY TO 'GET ROUND' GOD BY DOING THE 'RIGHT THINGS' WHEN MY HEART IS FAR FROM HIM?

ASK GOD TO FORGIVE YOU FOR THESE TIMES AND HELP YOU TO BE WILLING TO OBEY HIM HOWEVER YOU ARE FEELING.

ISAIAH 6

WE HAVE HAD A TASTE OF THE KIND OF MESSAGE ISAIAH HAS BEEN GIVEN. NOW WE ARE 'BACK-TRACKING' TO SEE WHERE HE GOT IT FROM.

A TASTE OF ...

The last verses of chapter 5 (verse 26 onwards) described a vision of what our world calls power: marching ranks of soldiers. But in his vision of God, Isaiah sees real power. Uzziah, the king corrupted by pride, dies, but God is King for ever. Even the sound of the voices of his servants is like an earthquake (v 4).

Once Isaiah sees the purity and power of God, he knows he is in big trouble (v 5). So are we! But forgiveness is near (vs 6,7).

Forgiven and clean, Isaiah can now hear the call of God as never before (v 8). God tells him his task won't be easy – the people won't listen (v 9). They are so rebellious that the message will make them worse – but they must be told.

Yet at the end when it seems the nation is totally destroyed, there will be left a stump of a tree which is still holy (v 13). Even in our disasters, God reigns.

Ask God to give you the same willingness that Isaiah shows in verse 8, to answer his call.

ACTION

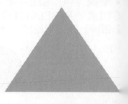

• SPEND SOME TIME IN PRAYER ASKING GOD TO MAKE YOU CLEAN AND HOLY. PRAY THAT EVERY ASPECT OF YOUR LIFE WILL BRING GLORY TO GOD.

ISAIAH 5:1-7, 26-30

WHAT IMPRESSION DO YOU HAVE SO FAR OF GOD'S MESSAGE TO HIS PEOPLE THROUGH ISAIAH? THE FIRST HALF OF THIS READING SHOULD PUT THAT RIGHT. SOME BIBLE TRANSLATIONS CALL IT A 'LOVE SONG' AND THAT'S EXACTLY WHAT IT IS.

• Who is the loving vineyard-keeper?
• Who is the beloved vineyard?

Imagine the agony of a lover who must threaten destruction to the one he loves. He must threaten to remove the hedge (v 5), taking away what marks out his beloved as belonging to him, and gives safety and protection. As there is no inward difference between Israel and Judah and their God-less neighbours, there will be no outward difference.

Why did God have to make these threats? Take a look at verses 8, 11, 19-23. Israel/Judah was a selfish consumer society, cynical, rejecting the standards of God. Remind you of any society you know?

What a contrast the Assyrian soldiers, described in verses 26-30, are to this. They've got sacrificial commitment to a cause, dedication and discipline. These qualities always win. A Communist once said, 'That's why we Communists will win in the end – your Christian ideology is better than ours, but we are more committed.'

ACTION

• THINK BACK OVER HOW YOU CAME TO CHRIST. CAN YOU SEE GOD TAKING TENDER CARE OVER YOU AS THE VINEYARD-KEEPER IN THE STORY DID OVER HIS VINEYARD (VS 2,3)? HOW MUCH COMMITMENT HAS HE HAD FROM YOU IN RESPONSE?

ISAIAH 10:5-27

IN RECENT HISTORY THE NEAREST WE HAVE KNOWN TO THE ASSYRIAN EMPIRE WAS THE NAZI EMPIRE. LIKE THE THIRD REICH, ASSYRIA ROSE FAST TO DOMINATE THE WORLD STAGE. ITS ARMIES WERE MARKED BY DISCIPLINE, RUTHLESSNESS AND FEROCITY. THEY HAD ABSOLUTE LOYALTY TO THEIR LEADER AND TOTAL DEDICATION TO THE CAUSE: GOOD QUALITIES TWISTED TO EVIL PURPOSES.

ABSOLUTE LOYALTY.

In their pride Assyria took all the credit for their own success (vs 13,14). But God is the Lord of history. He can use the strong and vicious even though they do not know they are being used (v 15). That doesn't make their vicious methods right – just as they have ruthlessly destroyed nations, they themselves will be destroyed (v 12). Like a fever or a forest fire (v 16), God's punishment will turn on those he has used to punish his people.

Even though Assyria oppressed them, there were some in Judah who looked to Assyria for political support against other countries. Some people will always gang up with the strongest. But God promises that after the time of oppression, a 'faithful few' will come back to him (vs 20,21).

When you look at the newspaper or watch the TV news, does it all look hopeless? It isn't. Satan may be the 'prince of this world', but God is still in overall control, and he knows what he is doing. Praise God for that

ACTION

• OVER THE NEXT COUPLE OF WEEKS READ THE NEWSPAPER OR WATCH THE NEWS ON TELEVISION. PICK OUT STORIES WHICH REALLY STRIKE YOU AS NEEDING PRAYER. YOU MAY WANT TO DO IT FOR A LONGER PERIOD OF TIME. IF YOU DO WHY DON'T YOU START KEEPING A SCRAP BOOK/JOURNAL OF THE NEWS STORIES AND WHAT YOU PRAYED FOR THEM.

DAYZD 65

CHECK OUT

ISAIAH 30:1-18

A USEFUL FRIEND.

THREATENED BY ASSYRIA, THE REACTION OF KING HEZEKIAH AT ONE STAGE WAS TO TURN TO EGYPT FOR SUPPORT. EGYPT WAS A GREAT AND POWERFUL EMPIRE, SO A USEFUL FRIEND. JUDAH'S AMBASSADORS MADE LONG JOURNEYS THROUGH DANGEROUS COUNTRY, WITH EXPENSIVE GIFTS FOR EGYPT (V 6).

But Egypt was an empire built on slavery, ruled by kings whose people saw them as gods. God regarded Israel's reliance on Egypt as an insult to him.

The message of verses 1–5 is simple: this world's help will fail you when you most need it.

How do the people react to God's warning about Egypt (vs 9-11)?

What will be the result of their reliance on Egypt (vs 12-14)?

What is their only real hope (v 15)?

Be honest! Do you ever build your hopes on anything other than God? Tick any of the sentences that apply to you:

Everything would be all right if only ...

- I had the right boyfriend/girlfriend.
- I had the right job.
- I were better looking.
  I were cleverer.
  I lived somewhere else.

Ask God to help you rely on him and nothing else.

ACTION

LOOK BACK TO EARLIER IN THIS BOOK (EXODUS) WHEN WE LOOKED AT MOSES GUIDING GOD'S PEOPLE OUT OF EGYPT AND INTO FREEDOM. HOW DID THEY REACT WHEN THEY HAD ESCAPED? THANKFUL?

ASK GOD TO FORGIVE YOU FOR THE TIMES WHEN YOU THINK YOU KNOW BETTER THAN HE DOES.

ISAIAH 36:1-22

EVER BEEN INVOLVED IN A CONVERSATION WITH A NON-CHRISTIAN ABOUT YOUR FAITH, IN WHICH THE OTHER PERSON SEEMS DETERMINED TO 'WIN THE ARGUMENT'? THEY BATTER YOU WITH POINT AFTER POINT, AND GRADUALLY YOU LOSE CONFIDENCE IN YOUR OWN ANSWERS, UNTIL YOU START TO WONDER WHY YOU BELIEVE AT ALL.

Something like that is happening here. Having conquered all the fortress cities of Judah (v 1), the mighty Sennacherib of Assyria comes to complete the job by reducing Jerusalem to rubble. His commander-in-chief is a master of propaganda, and with point after point he urges the Israelites to surrender:

THEY BATTER YOU WITH POINT AFTER POINT.

• Brave words alone are no good (vs 4,5).
• Egypt's support is useless (v 6).
• Your God is powerless (v 7).
• Your army is non-existent (v 8).
• It was your God who sent me to destroy you (v 10).

Points 1,2 and 4 are all true. Point 5 is only half the truth. Point 3 is his big mistake.

Sennacherib's historical records are curiously silent about what actually happened. A siege is described, then a withdrawal with ransom money – but no surrender. Unheard of!

Satan's message never changes – he ridicules our hope in God and denies God's power to help. The action described in verses 21,22 is often the best course – say nothing. And report everything to the King!

ACTION

• THINK OF ANYONE YOU KNOW WHO MAKES A HABIT OF ATTACKING YOUR FAITH. PRAY FOR WISDOM IN TALKING TO THAT PERSON. PRAY THAT YOU WILL TRUST AND BELIEVE THAT GOD IS IN CONTROL. PRAY FOR HIS GUIDANCE OVER THIS SITUATION.

DAYZD 67

ISAIAH 37:1-20

WHEN DO YOU THINK OUR FAITH GROWS MOST?
• WHEN WE'RE RECEIVING BLESSING AFTER BLESSING FROM GOD.
• WHEN THINGS ARE REALLY TOUGH.

ACTUALLY, BOTH ARE RIGHT.

OUR FAITH.

We need the times of blessing to show us that God really cares; but we also need the tough times to strengthen our trust. Often God can use the times of greatest pressure to produce his finest fruit in us.

With an enemy army outside the city and fear inside it, Hezekiah decides to make his repentance clear to God (v 1). He also enlists Isaiah's help (vs 2-4) and Isaiah is able immediately to send back encouragement (vs 5,6). God knows about the situation and has already made his plans (v 7, fulfilled in v 9a).

Sennacherib doesn't know that he is already doomed. So in his letter (vs 8-13) he struts like a peacock. He thinks he himself is God – the living representative of the god Asshur, national god of Assyria. To him all gods are the same – he has never considered the possibility that there might be a real, living God.

But Hezekiah, in his moment of greatest danger, rises to his finest confidence in God (vs 14-20). To him, God is not just the God of success; he is in charge even when disaster threatens.

ACTION

• READ VERSES 16 AND 17a CAREFULLY. WHAT DO THEY TEACH YOU ABOUT HOW TO PRAY IN A CRISIS?

ISAIAH 37:21-38

HOW SHOULD WE REACT TO THOSE WHO HAVE A
LAUGH AT THE EXPENSE OF CHRISTIANS?

- ATTACK THEM IN RETURN.
- LEAVE IT TO GOD TO DEAL WITH THEM.
- JOIN THEM.

HAVE A LAUGH.

Sennacherib has been boasting about all his marvellous victories, and laughing at God's people. God's answer to him through Isaiah begins today's reading (vs 21-29). His boasting was ridiculous, because it was all God's doing. God and his people can afford to laugh at Sennacherib (v 22).

As for Hezekiah, his faith is answered with the promise in verses 30–32. Why will God defend his people? Not because they are so good – we have already seen that they aren't. He defends them for his own honour (v 35) and because he has promised to do so.

God's action (v 36) shook even Sennacherib's confidence. But he never had the guts to admit that Israel's God was in charge. So this brilliant and powerful man died in darkness and sadness, killed by his own sons (v 38). Jesus' words in Matthew 26:52 are an appropriate comment on Sennacherib's end.

ACTION

- PRAY FOR PARTICULAR COUNTRIES THAT ARE RULED BY MILITARY DICTATORS OR UNJUST GOVERNMENTS. ASK GOD TO TRANSFORM THOSE SITUATIONS BY HIS LOVING POWER.

- 'I WON'T CHANGE – NOT UNLESS THE GEEZER WITH THE BIG BEARD LANDS DOWN IN FRONT OF ME AND PULLS A GIRAFFE OUT OF HIS NOSTRIL AND GOES, "I'M GOD"'
LIAM GALLAGHER, LEAD SINGER OF OASIS.

CHECK OUT

ISAIAH 39:1-8

LOOK BACK AT WHAT WE SAID ABOUT KING HEZEKIAH ON THE FIRST SECTION OF READINGS FROM ISAIAH. IN THE LAST FEW DAYS WE'VE MOSTLY SEEN HIS GOOD SIDE. BUT FOUR DAYS AGO WE ALSO HAD A GLIMPSE OF HIS FOOLISH SIDE: A TENDENCY TO TRUST IN POLITICAL ALLIANCES RATHER THAN IN GOD.

A GLIMPSE OF HIS FOOLISH SIDE:

After his glorious defiance of Sennacherib's army, this episode shows a completely different Hezekiah. Perhaps the threat that he might die (38:1) had robbed him of courage. Perhaps his recovery from illness, combined with the defeat of Sennacherib, made him stupidly confident.

Did he feel he was being terribly clever in acting in such a friendly way to the rising power of Babylon (soon to conquer Assyria)? Did he fancy himself playing international politics? Whatever the reason, he exposed all Judah's assets (v 2) to a nation which was soon to become Judah's greatest enemy.

Isaiah's prophecy in response to this (vs 5-7) should have made Hezekiah worried. But instead he took the same attitude as a much later French king was to take: 'After me, the flood'. In others words, 'I'm all right, Jack – never mind what happens afterwards'.

Even the best servant of God can be led astray by pride. Are you trusting too much in your own 'assets' – your abilities, or even your 'spiritual gifts'?

ACTION

• MAKE A LIST OF FIVE THINGS YOU THINK YOU ARE GOOD AT: SPORT, WRITING, GETTING ON WITH PEOPLE, ETC. OVER THE COMING WEEK TAKE EACH OF THOSE GIFTS IN TURN AND USE IT AS A FOCUS FOR YOUR PRAYERS.

• THANK GOD FOR GIVING YOU THE ABILITY TO DO THAT TASK WELL.
• SAY SORRY TO HIM FOR THINKING ARROGANTLY ABOUT THIS ABILITY.
• ASK HIM TO SHOW YOU HOW YOU CAN USE THIS GIFT FOR HIS GLORY AND NOT YOUR OWN.

ISAIAH 40:1-11

NOW FOR THE GOOD NEWS! WE'VE JUMPED A CENTURY AND A HALF (PROPHETS ARE ALLOWED TO DO THAT SORT OF THING). ISAIAH'S PREDICTION ABOUT BABYLON, WHICH WE READ IN CHAPTER 39, CAME TRUE IN 587 BC WHEN THE BABYLONIANS CONQUERED JERUSALEM AND CARRIED OFF THE JEWS AS EXILES. CHAPTER 40 IS A MESSAGE FOR THOSE EXILES.

The command comes in verses 3-5 to clear the way for the biggest highway ever: a motorway for the living God. Not only is this a message for the exiles in Babylon; much later John the Baptist also quoted these words to announce the coming of Jesus (John 1:23). When God rescues his people, all mankind will see his glory. But notice where the highway starts: in the desert, a place of pain and sorrow.

God's people are always called to be messengers of good news - the good news that there is no hope in mankind (vs 6,7). That's good news? Yes, because unlike peoples lives, the promises of God will never end (v 8).

PROPHETS ARE ALLOWED TO DO THAT SORT OF THING.

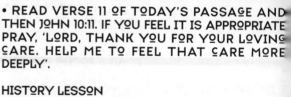

• READ VERSE 11 OF TODAY'S PASSAGE AND THEN JOHN 10:11. IF YOU FEEL IT IS APPROPRIATE PRAY, 'LORD, THANK YOU FOR YOUR LOVING CARE. HELP ME TO FEEL THAT CARE MORE DEEPLY'.

HISTORY LESSON
HISTORY REPEATS ITSELF.
HAS TO.
NO ONE LISTENS.

STEVE TURNER FROM *NICE AND NASTY*

ISAIAH 45:1-13

CAN YOU BEGIN TO SEE A PATTERN?

NON-BELIEVERS CAN DO GOD'S WORK.

• Israel disobeyed God.
• God allowed Assyria to oppress them.
• When the lesson had been learnt, God punished Assyria for their sins.

• Later Israel disobeys God again.
• God allows Babylon to invade Israel and deport the Jews.
• Now the lesson is learnt, God is going to punish Babylon.

God's chosen instrument is Cyrus, king of Persia. In 539 BC Cyrus defeated the Babylonian army and took control of their empire. The exiled Jews were allowed to return home.

In spite of the rebellion of man and the power of Satan, God is the Lord of creation. He still rules all things, and all the good and bad events of life are under his control. Behind the scenes of world politics today, God is still saying to the rulers and men and women of power, 'I raised you up, and I will throw you down'.

ACTION

• READ EZRA 1:1-4 TO FIND OUT WHAT CYRUS DID WHEN HE TOOK OVER. CYRUS WAS A PAGAN KING YET HE CARRIED OUT THE WORK OF GOD. DO YOU THINK NON-BELIEVERS CAN DO GOD'S WORK TODAY? TRY DISCUSSING THIS WITH OTHER CHRISTIANS. IT WILL HELP TO LOOK THROUGH A RECENT NEWSPAPER SO YOU CAN THINK ABOUT HOW GOD IS INVOLVED IN ACTUAL EVENTS.

ISAIAH 47:1-15

THINK OF THE MOST 'SUCCESSFUL' -
IN THE WORLD'S USE OF THE WORD -
PERSON (OR COUNTRY) THAT YOU
KNOW OF. ENVIOUS? BUT HOW LONG
DO YOU THINK THAT 'SUCCESS'
WILL LAST?

Without God, success brings greed, self-indulgence, cruelty. That stuff must eventually come under the judgment of God.

Like a beautiful, pure, young woman becoming an ageing prostitute; like a great queen turned into a dirty slave, the Babylonian empire is to be destroyed by God, says the prophet (vs 1-3). Occult powers, magic, astrology (vs 9-15) will not save her. Because she showed no mercy (v 6), none will be shown to her.

For God's people, there is a promise of freedom from oppression (v 4). Is this promise coming true for you? Write down the things God has freed you from, the things he is in the process of freeing you from, and the things you would like him to free you from. Thank him for what he has done already and ask him to help you wait patiently for what he will do.

ACTION

• DO YOU READ YOUR HOROSCOPES OR DABBLE IN THE OCCULT, EG OUIJA BOARDS OR MEDIUMS, TO FIND OUT WHAT YOUR FUTURE HOLDS? WELL DON'T! THE BIBLE MAKES IT CLEAR HOW EVIL GOD THINKS IT IS - LOOK UP THESE BIBLE VERSES: LEVITICUS 19:31, LEVITICUS 20:6; ISAIAH 8:19,20.

• ONLY THE LIVING GOD TRULY KNOWS THE FUTURE. ONLY A FOOL TRUSTS IN ANYTHING ELSE.

ISAIAH 2:1-5

WHERE WILL IT ALL END?

A FAMILIAR CRY! WE'RE BACK-TRACKING AGAIN TO FOLLOW ANOTHER STRAND IN ISAIAH'S PROPHECIES. WE'VE LOOKED AT HIS MESSAGE TO THE PEOPLE OF HIS OWN DAY, THREATENED BY ASSYRIA. WE'VE SEEN HIS MESSAGE TO A FUTURE ISRAEL WHICH WILL SUFFER EXILE IN BABYLON. NOW HERE IS A MESSAGE THAT LOOKS EVEN FURTHER AHEAD.

WE'RE BACK-TRACKING AGAIN.

Even before God's judgment falls on his people, we know the final outcome. God lifts Isaiah's eyes to the very end of history, to see things from his perspective. One day God's dwelling-place on earth – his own people – will be lifted high above all the nations of the earth. God will speak to all the earth, and the people will hear and obey.

But how should God's people respond to this hope? Sit back and wait for it all to happen? Verse 5 gives a different answer. Try putting it into your own words.

God knows how it'll all end!

ACTION

• ONE OF THE MOST ASKED QUESTIONS BY CHRISTIANS IS 'WHAT WILL HEAVEN BE LIKE?' 'WHAT WILL YOU HAVE TO DO ALL DAY?', 'WILL YOU HAVE MEMORIES?' LANCE PIERSON IN HIS BOOK *WHAT ABOUT IT?*, SCRIPTURE UNION, SHEDS SOME LIGHT ON THESE QUESTIONS. IT'S AN EXCELLENT RESOURCE SO MAKE SOME TIME AND READ IT!

ISAIAH 9:2-7

OKAY, ISAIAH, SO YOU SAY AT THE END OF HISTORY GOD IS GOING TO BRING UNIVERSAL PEACE AND JUSTICE. HOW'S HE GOING TO DO IT, THEN? TODAY'S PASSAGE ADDS A BIT MORE DETAIL TO THE PICTURE.

Galilee, the most northern area of Israel (see v 1) became the first territory to fall to the Assyrians. But God's message to those overtaken by this disaster was, 'The very people who are so dark and depressed at the moment will be the first to come into my sunshine' (v 2).

God's most powerful weapon is to be brought out: a baby boy, born to be King (vs 6,7). Where was the area Jesus started his teaching and healing? Galilee! See Matthew 4:12-16 for how this prophecy was fulfilled.

Jesus' kingdom has begun. It will grow for ever and never be spoiled by injustice or cruelty (v 7). God, the almighty Father, will establish a perfect kingdom at the end of time where Jesus will reign (Revelation 11:15). There's only one possible response to that – praise!

Look at the names Jesus is given here. 'Wonderful Counsellor' – so you can ask for his wisdom. 'Mighty God' – so you can rely on his strength and praise him for his power. 'Eternal Father' – so thank him that he has always loved you. 'Prince of Peace' – he gives peace to all who follow him. Ask him to give you the peace which comes from loving and obeying him.

UNIVERSAL PEACE.

ACTION

• TIME TO PRAISE GOD! LISTEN TO A WORSHIP SONG. THANK JESUS, THAT HIS LOVE FOR US IS SO GREAT!

CHECK OUT
ISAIAH 24:1-23

WHY ALL THIS DEVASTATION?

EVER SEEN PICTURES OF HIROSHIMA AFTER THE BOMB? THAT'S THE SCALE OF DESTRUCTION ISAIAH IS DESCRIBING HERE. THE WHOLE EARTH A WASTELAND, RIPPED APART BY EARTHQUAKES. MISERY IN THE COUNTRYSIDE (VS 6-9), RUIN IN THE CITIES (VS 10-12). DEPRESSION AFFECTING EVERYONE (V 11); NO ONE SPARED (V 2). WHY ALL THIS DEVASTATION? VERSE 5 GIVES THE ANSWER.

Nowadays a lot of people feel a bit uneasy about the idea of God's judgment. How does it make you feel?

• I find it impossible to believe.
• I think it makes God seem a bit of a tyrant.
• I believe in it, but I'm not altogether happy about it.
• I'm glad that one day God will destroy evil.
• I can't wait for God to crush all the bad guys.

In the last two readings we've been looking at the future kingdom of peace and justice which God is going to bring in. But we have to come to terms with the fact that it can't be done without destroying all that is evil in the earth. Verse 21 is the key verse – punishment of evil is a necessary condition for justice and peace.

But the picture isn't all bleak! Verses 14-16a offer hope to those who are left: the glory of God will shine in his people.

ACTION

• WHAT ARE YOU MOST AFRAID OF? ASK GOD TO SHOW YOU THAT YOU NEED NOT FEAR EVIL BECAUSE IT WILL ALL BE DESTROYED ONE DAY.

ISAIAH 25:1-9

'CONSIDER IT DONE!'

HAVE YOU EVER LOOKED FORWARD TO A MEAL SO MUCH THAT YOU CAN ALMOST TASTE IT EVEN BEFORE YOU BEGIN EATING? THE PROMISES OF GLORY AT THE END OF CHAPTER 24 ARE SO REAL TO ISAIAH THAT AS HE LOOKS FORWARD HE WRITES A HYMN OF PRAISE FOR PEOPLE TO SING WHEN IT'S ALL COMPLETED! AS FAR AS HE IS CONCERNED, WHATEVER GOD PROMISES HE WILL DO IS ALREADY DONE.

YOU CAN ALMOST TASTE IT ?

So the hymn in verses 1-5 is written from God's perspective – it looks back from the end of time. It is clear now that God always knew what he was doing and never abandoned his loving plan for human beings.

The great fortress cities, the power bases of oppressive empires, are destroyed (vs 2,3). The downtrodden masses – the poor, starved, dispossessed and oppressed – have found shelter (v 4). The bloodthirsty shouts of the violent have been silenced (v 5).

Three great blessings are promised:
• A great feast – all the hungry will be fed with the best (v 6).
• At last the cloud of darkness and fear that hides God from people will be lifted (v 7 – see 2 Corinthians 4:3,4).
• No more death! No more suffering or sorrow (v 8).

God's people will be shown to be right; their trust in God will see its reward.

ACTION

• YOU WILL BE A PART OF THIS! HOW DOES THAT MAKE YOU FEEL? IF YOU KEEP A PRAYER JOURNAL, WRITE DOWN WHAT YOUR THOUGHTS ARE AND COMMIT THEM TO GOD.

• COMPARE THE OLD TESTAMENT PICTURE OF GOD'S ULTIMATE PURPOSE FOR HIS PEOPLE WITH THE NEW TESTAMENT PICTURE IN REVELATION 7:15-17, 21:1-4.

ISAIAH 52:13-53:12

WE'VE SEEN TWO SIDES TO ISAIAH'S VISION OF THE FUTURE - JUDGMENT AND GLORY. NOW WE SEE TWO SIDES TO HIS VISION OF THE ONE THROUGH WHOM GOD WILL CARRY OUT PLANS. THREE SECTIONS AGO WE LOOKED AT HIS VISION OF A BOY BORN TO BE KING. TODAY WE SEE THAT KING AS 'THE SUFFERING SERVANT'. THIS IS ONE OF FOUR PASSAGES IN ISAIAH THAT PREDICT GOD'S SENDING OF A SERVANT WHO WILL SUFFER FOR HIS PEOPLE. JESUS FULFILLED THEM ALL IN DETAIL.

The loser lifted up (52:13-15)
The servant of God must succeed in the end. Through torment and pain he will come to shatter the values of the powerful.

An unpretentious life (53:1-3)
Not a mighty tree – more like a young plant. And a plant mostly made up of root (v 2). Tenacious, tough and full of hidden power below the surface.

Suffering for others (53:4-6)
Both words used in verse 54 have more than one meaning: suffering/sicknesses and sorrow/pain. The sacrifice of Jesus will heal all the results of humankind's fall.

Tragic death (53:7-9)
Jesus was silent before all his accusers: the Jewish Council, Pilate, Herod. In spite of his pain he said nothing. He acted like a lamb going to the slaughterhouse (see John 1:29).

Glorious victory (53:10-12)
His death looked like a tragic mistake, but God was in control all the time. And because of that death, forgiveness will come to millions.

ACTION

• READ THROUGH THE LYRICS OF THIS SONG. IF YOU FEEL IT IS APPROPRIATE, USE IT AS THE BASIS TO LEAD INTO PRAYER.

THANK YOU FOR SAVING ME WHAT CAN I SAY?
YOU ARE MY EVERYTHING I WILL SING YOUR PRAISE.
YOU SHED YOUR BLOOD FOR ME WHAT CAN I SAY?
YOU TOOK MY SIN AND SHAME, A SINNER CALLED BY NAME.

Martin Smith
© 1993 Curious? Music UK/Kingsway's Thankyou Music/MCPS used by permission.

ISAIAH 61:1-11

'DON'T YOU KNOW THERE WILL BE NO LAUGHING IN HEAVEN?' SO SAID A NINETEENTH-CENTURY MINISTER ONCE. WHAT RUBBISH - BUT MANY PEOPLE BELIEVE CHRISTIANITY IS A RECIPE FOR MISERY - AND OFTEN SOME CHRISTIANS HELP THEM BELIEVE! BUT LOOK AT THE EFFECT OF GOD'S PROMISED DELIVERER:

NO LAUGHING IN HEAVEN ?

• His rescue and healing of the oppressed and poor will completely re-structure society (vs 1-4)
• The world will beat a path to the door of God's people to share their happiness (vs 5-7).
• At last injustice will be ended. God's people will be the most liberated and the happiest of all (vs 8,9).
• The love affair of God and his people will be obvious to all. The world will be like a vast wedding reception (vs 10,11).

Jesus quoted these words from Isaiah in his very first public sermon (see Luke 4:16-19). Unlike the 'servant songs' which were only understood fully after Jesus' death, this had always been seen as a prophecy about the Messiah. So Jesus was saying 'I'm the one who will make all this come true'.

• HOW DO YOU THINK THE CHURCH CAN HELP BRING 'GOOD NEWS' TO THOSE WHO ARE REALLY POOR, AND 'FREEDOM' TO THOSE WHO ARE IN PRISON? BY GIVING THEM A FAITH THAT WILL HELP THEM PUT UP WITH THEIR TROUBLES? OR BY FIGHTING THE INJUSTICE THAT CAUSES THEIR PROBLEMS? OR BOTH? TRY DISCUSSING THIS WITH OTHER CHRISTIANS. TALK IT THROUGH WITH GOD AS WELL. ASK HIM TO SHOW YOU WAYS WHERE YOU OR OTHERS CAN HELP.

ISAIAH 49:1-7

ONE OF THE BIGGEST FAILINGS OF ISRAEL THROUGHOUT HISTORY WAS TO THINK THAT GOD WAS FOR THEM ALONE. THEY WEREN'T GOING TO SHARE HIS BLESSINGS WITH THOSE OTHER WICKED NATIONS!

TOTAL CONFIDENCE.

This passage is one of many directed against that mistake. It's a bit like the ripples caused by dropping a stone into water. The prophet's call (v 1) becomes the call to Israel (v 3), then the call to the world (v 6) and it ends with the despised servant of God glorified by all the nations (v 7).

Actually, we're dealing with a sort of 'double exposure' here; one picture superimposed on top of another. Verses 1 and 2 could be talking about Isaiah himself. Or we could be once again sharing a vision of Jesus, the supreme servant of God. Either way, there's total confidence here. God's call started long before his servant was born (vs 1,5). Nothing can stop God's work being done (v 7). And there's no room for exclusiveness: the great aim is to see the whole world saved (v 6).

Are there people you'd rather not share God's Kingdom with? Confess this to God and ask him to change your attitudes.

ACTION

CHECK OUT JOHN 20:21. IN WHAT WAYS DO YOU THINK ALL CHRISTIANS CAN SHARE IN THE SERVANT'S TASK? ASK GOD TO MAKE YOU A SERVANT WILLING TO DO HIS WORK.

ISAIAH 63:15-64:12

AFTER THE 'SPIRITUAL UPLIFT' OF
SUNDAY, DOES THAT OLD FEELING OF
DEPRESSION CREEP BACK ON MONDAY
MORNING? DO YOU LOOK
BACK WITH REGRET TO
THE FIRST JOYFUL DAYS
OF YOUR CHRISTIAN LIFE
AND WONDER WHY IT
SEEMS SUCH HARD
GOING NOW?

SUCH HARD GOING.

Isaiah has had glorious visions
of good things to come, but
he's still got to live with the
problems of his own time. This
is a prayer of desperation and
confusion, but above all an
honest prayer in which Isaiah
speaks out the mixed feelings
of the Jews.

'Have you forgotten us, Lord? Don't you care any more? Why do you let us keep
on making the same mistakes (63:17)? It's as if we never belonged to you (63:19)!
Sound like any of your prayers? 'Why am I so weak, Lord? Am I a real Christian at
all?'

But when God did show his power (64:1-3) the people said, 'He frightens us –
don't let him talk to us' (see Exodus 20:19-21). You can't have it both ways!

From verse 5 on, we're getting down to the root of the problem. God's people
had hidden their real selves from him. Now, in a moving confession, they admit
how weak they really are. 'Lord, we are no good, and now we've got nothing. It's
what we deserve. Even so, because you are good, remember us.'

God understands us better than we understand ourselves. Above all, seek to
make your prayers honest and trust that God, who was with you yesterday, will
be with you today and tomorrow.

• MAKE SURE THAT YOU MEET WITH
GOD REGULARLY THROUGH PRAYER,
ATTENDING CHURCH, AND THROUGH
BIBLE STUDY. IF YOU WANT GOD TO
GUIDE YOU, MAKE SURE YOU ARE IN
TOUCH WITH HIM TO HEAR WHAT HE
IS SAYING TO YOU!

CHECK OUT

ISAIAH 65:1-8, 17-25

THE CHEEK.

HERE IS GOD'S ANSWER TO THE PRAYER IN CHAPTERS 63-64. 'IF YOU HAD PRAYED, I WOULD HAVE LISTENED. I WAITED FOR YOU, BUT YOU WENT OFF IN THE OPPOSITE DIRECTION. AND THEN YOU HAD THE CHEEK TO PRETEND YOU WERE BETTER THAN HONEST UNBELIEVERS (V 5)! YOU WON'T GET AWAY WITH IT (V 6).'

But God's purpose in punishment is always to rescue whatever he can. He always acts in love. So verses 17-25 repeat his promise of a new world. It will be a place of happiness (vs 17-19), health (v 20), success and fulfilment (vs 23,24), safety (v 25).

Isaiah's prophecies are a bit like a tapestry woven with light and dark threads; or a symphony with themes in major and minor keys. Judgment and promise, destruction and restoration, despair and hope alternate with each other. But the major key always ends the symphony, and the light threads form the final picture. The last word is always one of promise and hope. The Kingdom of God is coming.

Write down the most important message or messages that reading Isaiah has brought home to you. Is there something you can thank God for? pray about? do something about? tell others about?

ACTION

LOOK AT THE LYRICS FROM THIS BRILLIANT SONG BY JONNY BAKER 'YOU HAVE RESCUED ME':

LACKED PURPOSE DIRECTION AND MEANING
COULDN'T MAKES SENSE OF LIVING IN THIS WORLD
EACH WAY I TURNED THERE SEEMED NO SOLUTION
THEN YOU CAME AND RESCUED ME.
© 1994 Serious Music UK, 11 Junction Road, Bath, Avon, BA2 3NQ. Used by permission.

ASK GOD TO SHOW YOU HIS PURPOSE AND DIRECTION FOR YOUR LIFE.

2 TIMOTHY 3:1-5

WHAT'S THE WORLD COMING TO?

WHAT ARE 'THE LAST DAYS'? IT DOESN'T MEAN THAT THE END OF THE WORLD WILL NECESSARILY COME NEXT FRIDAY AFTERNOON! ALL THE THINGS MENTIONED HERE HAVE BEEN HAPPENING SINCE THE TIME PAUL WROTE TO TIMOTHY. JESUS DESCRIBES THEM AS 'THE FIRST PAINS OF CHILDBIRTH' (MARK 13:8) – THEY MEAN THAT SOMETHING NEW IS COMING. BECAUSE THESE THINGS ARE TAKING PLACE WE KNOW WE ARE ALL LIVING IN THE LAST STAGE OF HISTORY.

Often people say, 'I don't know what the world is coming to'. You do! You know that these things will get worse and worse as people continue to rebel against God.

Paul wants Timothy not to worry about these things or get caught up with what rebellious people are doing. Instead, he should:

• keep to God's truth (v 14).
• let God's word train him in holiness (vs 15-17).

ACTION

• FIND TODAY'S NEWSPAPERS AND PRAY ABOUT ONE BAD SITUATION IN THE WORLD.

LORD, YOU ARE CALLING
THE PEOPLE OF YOUR KINGDOM,
TO BATTLE IN YOUR NAME AGAINST THE ENEMY.
TO STAND BEFORE YOU,
A PEOPLE WHO WILL SERVE YOU, TILL YOUR KINGDOM IS RELEASED THROUGHOUT THE EARTH.

LET YOUR KINGDOM COME,
LET YOUR WILL BE DONE
ON EARTH AS IT IS IN HEAVEN.

AT THE NAME OF JESUS
EVERY KNEE MUST BOW.
THE DARKNESS OF THIS AGE MUST FLEE AWAY.
RELEASE YOUR POWER
TO FLOW THROUGHOUT THE LAND,
LET YOUR GLORY BE REVEALED AS WE PRAISE.

Simon and Lorraine Fenner
© 1989 Kingsway's Thankyou Music/MCPS. Used by permission.

THESSALONIANS 2:1-12

AS THE WORLD APPROACHES THE 'DAY OF THE LORD', THE DAY WHEN JESUS WILL RETURN, THE BATTLE BETWEEN GOOD AND EVIL BECOMES MORE OBVIOUS. AT THE END, SATAN, THE ENEMY OF GOD, WILL SHOW HIMSELF IN HIS TRUE COLOURS. THESE SCRIPTURES SHOW US SOMETHING OF WHAT WILL HAPPEN:

• Evil will continue to the end (v 3).
• The supreme effort of Satan is still to come (v 4).
• Evil will challenge good and show itself through a person who draws his power from Satan (v 9).
• Many will be deceived by this power (vs 10,11) – but only those who have already rejected God's truth.
• The wicked one will be destroyed by Jesus (v 8).
• Evil is destined for hell (v 3).

THE BATTLE BETWEEN GOOD AND EVIL.

How can you avoid being deceived by evil? Check out John 8:31,32 and James 1:5. Pray that God will keep you strong against temptation. Thank him that he is in control of the future.

ACTION

READ THROUGH THESE LYRICS AND THEN SPEND SOME TIME MEDITATING ON THEM.

WE WILL TEAR DOWN EVERY STRONGHOLD
THROUGH THE POWER OF HIS WORD.
WE WILL SEEK TO BRING HIS KINGDOM IN,
MAKE A WAY FOR ITS RETURN.

WE WILL TELL OF HIS SALVATION,
FOR THE CHURCH OF CHRIST IS CALLED
TO BRING HEALING TO THE NATIONS,
SEE HIS RIGHTEOUSNESS RESTORED.

SATAN IS DEFEATED,
CHRIST HAS OVERCOME, SEATED AT THE FATHER'S HAND,
LORD, ON EARTH MAY YOUR WILL NOW BE DONE.

Dave Bilbrough
© 1991 Kingsway's Thankyou Music/MCPS. Used by permission.

DAY'Z'D 84

REVELATION 5:1-14

LIVING IN EXILE BECAUSE OF HIS FAITH, JOHN HAS A VISION OF JESUS RULING AND REIGNING IN THE MIDDLE OF THE UNIVERSE. IT IS JESUS WHO IS ON GOD'S THRONE. HE IS THE ONE IN THE SEAT OF AUTHORITY.

No one is found worthy to open God's book and reveal his secrets except one man who is seen as two creatures:

THE SEAT OF AUTHORITY.

• A lion (v 5): This speaks of strength and kingship.

• A lamb (v 6): Jesus is the Lamb of God who takes away the sins of the world by his death on the cross (John 1:29).

Everything worships and serves the Lamb:

• The twenty-four elders who stand for the people of God (they are described in 4:4).

• The four living creatures (who are listed in 4:7): lion, greatest of wild animals; man, greatest of created beings; bull, greatest of domestic animals; eagle, greatest of birds.

When Jesus comes to rule, the whole universe will worship him.

ACTION

• SPEND SOME TIME PRAISING AND WORSHIPPING JESUS THE KING. READ THROUGH THE LYRICS OF THIS SONG. WHAT DO THE WORDS SAY TO YOU? THANK GOD THAT YOUR FUTURE BELONGS TO HIM.

I'M COMING UP THE MOUNTAIN, LORD;
I'M SEEKING YOU AND YOU ALONE.
I KNOW THAT I WILL BE TRANSFORMED,
MY HEART UNVEILED BEFORE YOU ...

I'M COMING TO WORSHIP,
I'M COMING TO BOW DOWN,
I'M COMING TO MEET WITH YOU.

Matt Redman
© 1995 Kingsway's Thankyou Music (From Worship Together Vol 14). Used b
permission.

REVELATION 18:1-24

BABYLON HAS ALWAYS BEEN A PICTURE OF OPPOSITION TO THE KINGDOM OF GOD. THIS GREAT CITY IN MESOPOTAMIA WAS THE CENTRE OF PAGAN LIFE; LATER ITS NAME WAS USED FOR THE EQUALLY WICKED CITY OF ROME. AS IT HAS FALLEN IN THE PAST (ISAIAH 21:9) AND BEEN DEFEATED BY THE CROSS, SO IT WILL BE TOTALLY DESTROYED IN THE FUTURE. JOHN IS PREDICTING THE FALL OF THE ROMAN EMPIRE BUT ALSO THE FINAL DESTRUCTION OF EVIL.

THE FINAL DESTRUCTION OF EVIL.

In verses 11-17, John is writing of ordinary everyday business trading. Even that will be judged one day.

All God's people who have been martyred over the years of history will be avenged (v 24).

What should our reaction be to the punishment of evil (v 20)?

What should our attitude be to evil people?

ACTION

• CHECK OUT ISAIAH 13 AND 47; JEREMIAH 50 AND 51; EZEKIEL 27 TO SEE THE PROPHECIES AND VISIONS JOHN REFERS TO IN THE OLD TESTAMENT. ISN'T IT AMAZING THAT THE GUIDANCE AND VISION GOD SPEAKS ABOUT IN THE OLD TESTAMENT IS, AND WILL BE FULFILLED. THANK GOD THAT HE IS SOMEONE WHO STANDS BY HIS WORD.

DAYZD 86

REVELATION 21:1-8

A NEW HEAVEN AND EARTH TO EXPLORE.

SOME PEOPLE HAVE THE IDEA THAT IN HEAVEN THERE WILL BE NOTHING TO DO. BUT THERE WILL BE A NEW HEAVEN AND EARTH TO EXPLORE FOR STARTERS! GOD MAKES ALL THINGS NEW!

God will live with his people (v 3). That has always been his intention and promise.

• In Exodus 19:20-22, God comes to his people on the mountain but they can't touch it or they will die because of his holiness.

• He then comes and lives in a tent among them as they travel into the promised land. Then he lets them build a temple as his 'house'.

• Finally, in Jesus he lives in this world as a human being himself. Through the cross the way is opened for God to live in our lives. But still our experience of him is limited.

• In the future he will be with us always and pain will cease (v 4). We will be able to experience his life power to the full (v 6).

Why can we believe these things? Read 2 Corinthians 1:19-22.

ACTION

• SPEND SOME TIME THINKING ABOUT WHAT YOU WANT HEAVEN TO BE LIKE. DO YOU HAVE CONCERNS ABOUT GOING THERE? TALK TO GOD ABOUT THESE NOW.

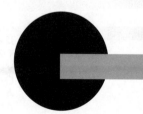

• CHECK OUT DAVID LAWRENCE'S EXCELLENT BOOK *HEAVEN ... IT'S NOT THE END OF THE WORLD!*, (SCRIPTURE UNION) TO FIND OUT MORE ON WHAT THE BIBLE TEACHES ABOUT HEAVEN. (DAVID IS ALSO AUTHOR OF *CHOCOLATE TEAPOT* AND *SUPERGLUE SANDWICH*, BOTH AVAILABLE FROM SCRIPTURE UNION.)

2 PETER 3:1-10

I'M AMAZED HOW SOME PEOPLE TRY TO WORK OUT THE EXACT DATE WHEN JESUS IS COMING AGAIN. THEY SET A TIME, AND WHEN IT PASSES BY, BLINDLY SET ANOTHER ONE.

THE EXACT DATE WHEN JESUS IS COMING AGAIN.

Peter says that the day when Jesus comes will arrive like a thief. Does a thief ring you up and tell you he is coming? Of course not!

What are the arguments the scoffers use in verse 3. What is the best defence against them (v 2).

Two things to know from verse 9;

• He is definitely coming.
• He wants all to turn from sin.

What should your reaction be to those who ask mocking questions (v 4)?

Check out vs 5-7. How do the words and actions of God in the past assure us that in the future he will again do what he has said.

Is there a similarity between the people in Noah's day and our own (Matthew 24:37-39)?

ACTION

• WHEN THINGS GET TOUGH CHRISTIANS SOMETIMES LONG FOR CHRIST TO COME AGAIN AND FOR THEM TO JOIN HIM IN HEAVEN. AS WE SEE FROM THIS PASSAGE THE TIME WILL COME WHEN THIS WILL HAPPEN. BUT WHY IS THIS DAY SLOW IN COMING (V 9)? CHECK OUT EZEKIEL 18:23,32 TO FIND OUT WHAT GOD'S REASONS ARE FOR WAITING. THANK HIM THAT BECAUSE OF HIS LOVE FOR US, HE IS SLOW TO COME BACK TO EARTH.

2 PETER 3:11-18

DAYZD 89
EIGHTY NINE

WHAT KIND OF PEOPLE DO WE NEED TO BE IF WE ARE TO BE READY FOR HIS COMING?

THE COURAGE TO TALK.

• Holy and dedicated to God (v 11).
• Pure, faultless and at peace with God (v 14).
• On our guard (v 17).
• Growing in Christ (v 18).

It looks like a recipe for being perfect, doesn't it? Look at verse 15. In a sense we are already saved because we have given our lives to him. In another sense our 'being saved' is now being worked out. Jesus, at work in us, is producing holiness, purity and all the other qualities needed in our lives. When Jesus comes our salvation will be complete. When it is complete and we come to heaven we will easily fit in because we will be at home (v 13).

'The end of the world is near.' Sounds like a gloomy message! Do you think Christians are pessimists?

ACTION

• LISTEN TO REM'S SONG 'IT'S THE END OF THE WORLD AS WE KNOW IT.' TRY AND WRITE YOUR OWN LYRICS TO THIS SONG FROM A CHRISTIAN POINT OF VIEW. WHAT DO YOU FEEL ABOUT THE END OF THE WORLD FROM WHAT YOU HAVE READ IN THE BIBLE? DO YOU FEEL FINE?

• IT'S IMPORTANT TO TELL OTHER PEOPLE ABOUT YOUR FAITH. PRAY THAT GOD WILL GIVE YOU THE COURAGE TO TALK TO PEOPLE YOU KNOW WHO DON'T YET KNOW HIM.

• CHECK OUT *DAYZD: EVANGELISM* FOR HANDY TIPS ON TALKING TO PEOPLE ABOUT YOUR FAITH

PROVERBS 3:5-7

GUIDANCE IS A HUGE SUBJECT TO LOOK AT - IT COVERS SO MANY DIFFERENT THINGS. TAKE SOME TIME NOW TO THINK ABOUT THE DIFFERENT ASPECTS OF GUIDANCE YOU HAVE READ ABOUT IN *DAYZD*.

If you have been keeping a journal, look back over your notes and then look at these questions. If you haven't been keeping a journal look at the questions anyway:

• What different ways of seeking God's guidance have you learnt about through using *DAYZD*?

• What are the most exciting Bible passages you have read, and why?

• What are the most challenging Bible passages you have read, and why?

• How do you think you can seek God's guidance better?

• What do you still find difficult about following God and knowing his will? Spend some time in prayer, asking God to help you with these areas of your life.

ACTION

CHECK OUT PROVERBS 3:5-7. THESE VERSES REALLY SUM UP THE BEST WAYS TO GET TO KNOW GOD'S WILL IN ANY SITUATION. SPEND SOME TIME MEDITATING ON THESE VERSES. PRAY THAT WITH EVERY DECISION YOU HAVE TO MAKE YOU WILL CHECK IT OUT WITH GOD FIRST.

WRITE TO *DAYZD* AT SCRIPTURE UNION AND TELL US WHAT YOU LIKED AND DISLIKED ABOUT IT.

GET

DAY'ZD

AND YOU WON'T BE CONFUSED

- DOES GOD TALK TO NORMAL PEOPLE?
- ARE YOU A CHRISTIAN? GET A LIFE!
- I BELIEVE! WHERE TO NOW?
- SO WHAT'S RIGHT WITH SEX?

DAY'ZD GIVES IT TO YOU STRAIGHT FROM THE BIBLE.

90 DAYS FOR 90'S LIFE